Endorse

M000074714

In this book, one of several we have read of hers, Nancy has captured the essence of how God cares for every human being, regardless of whether they know it or not! It is a beautiful picture of the power in your name, the intimacy of relationship which is so beautifully crafted by Nancy through the use of Scripture, her poems, and actual stories of encounters supplemented by stories from God's Word, crafted with reflections, and questions that help us engage with God's Word and apply to our personal lives!

Nancy has, as we have experienced personally with her in ministry, the gift of knowing how to enter into a conversation with a stranger, that often leads to a salvation decision on the spot. She exudes "Salt & Light"! Her book expresses what she believes and lives, loving God passionately and others tangibly.

—Rick and Jayne Brekelbaum
Sr. Advisor of the International Orality Network

This book is pure Nancy Wilson – Insightful and profound, winsome and funny, motivating and challenging, with live stories. Nancy does through this book what she does on a daily basis. I am glad I was fully trained by her in StoryWave Evangelism.

After undergoing her training, my ministry in the Lord has never been the same both in universities and high schools, that we reach out to in Uganda. I now train all my disciples in Story-Wave! Telling the stories of Jesus is the easiest way of reaching out and connect to one's heartbeat. Nancy does, through this book, what she does with me as a friend; lovingly but persistently prods me to keep growing and telling stories of Jesus Christ until I see Him face to face in glory!

—Alex Turyagumanawe, African missionary discipling the next generation with LIFE Ministry Uganda

*Wow! Nancy's latest book **He Knows You by Name** is so beautifully crafted and written to engage the reader and lead him or her into a deeper intimacy with Jesus.*

The testimonies within, of the divine encounters Nancy has experienced around the world, is a witness to how believers should walk in boldness and fulfill the mission we have been called to; share the Gospel of Jesus Christ with everyone we encounter. As I read each story, it's likes Nancy's words had life and I could feel her emotions. With a smile on my face, I couldn't put down the book wanting to hear more!

I love how the Holy Spirit uses Nancy to weave the Bible stories and her own personal testimony into this beautiful tapestry that welcomes and embraces her audience into a personal relationship with Jesus.

*This book will certainly challenge you to self-reflection, and to step out in faith with expectancy. God wants to do amazing things through your life and empower you to live out your purpose, for **He Knows You by Name**!*

—**Stephanie de Oliveira**, Missions Pastor
Calvario City Church, Orlando FL

I have known Nancy Wilson for many years. There are few people as excited about the Lord and as prone to share Him with others as Nancy is. When you are around her you sense the unmistakable presence of Jesus.

—**Steve Douglass**, President of Cru

I love stories, and Nancy Wilson is a master storyteller, especially when they are stories about people encountering Jesus. Nancy winsomely engages almost everyone she meets, discovering who they are and telling them there is a God who knows them by name. You will be surprised, encouraged and motivated!

—**Judy Douglass**, Director, Cru Women's Resources
Writer, Speaker, Encourager

*There cannot be a more important subject than Nancy Wilson's book **He Knows You by Name**. I believe that God will use the writings in this book to draw you into the place of knowing Him more as you experience both the character of our Loving God, and our amazing new identity because of what He has done for us. Prepare to be blown away by the lover of your soul through this book!*

   —**Chris Vennetti**, Co-Founder, Disciple Nations International
   Author of "Journey into the Spirit Empowered Life"

Nancy is one of this generation's ambassadors from Jesus Christ on the earth. Her great faith and love for the Lord and her deep daily search for God, prepares her to explain more about the intimacy and great love of God towards His people. I am delighted to be associated with her both as my spiritual mum and in evangelism ministry for many years. Her life has been used by the Lord to inspire me daily. I believe after reading this wonderful book, you will experience an intimate relationship with our King Jesus.

   —**James Kintu**, Senior Pastor Grace and Glory Chapel
   Associate Director Chosen With A Mission Ministries -
   UGANDA - U.S.A.

Following Jesus' example as His chosen disciple, Nancy uses the stories in the Bible in a delightful and refreshing way to capture the hearts of those she encounters.

   In her book, Nancy shares her experiences, in response to her Master's direction, of connecting the hearts of those whose name He knows to His love and forgiveness. Nancy also challenges her readers to listen to the Shepherd's call, as they walk through life, and take the opportunities He presents to reach out to His chosen lost sheep.

   —**Marcia Pershall**, Action-Impact co-founder
   Pastor's wife, mother, grandmother (of 20)

*Nancy Wilson does it again. **He Knows You by Name** is a must read for every person. She has the most amazing way to use your name to connect one to a living God who cares about you. A marvelous witnessing tool!*

—Josh and Dottie McDowell
Speaker/Authors

For years I've defined Christian discipleship as "intimacy with Christ in his supremacy filling us with expectancy" (based on Colossians 1:27). There is no Christian leader I've met anywhere on planet earth who understands what biblical "intimacy" with King Jesus looks like the way Nancy Wilson does. She lives it. She teaches it. She inflames it in others. Now she digs into it with us in this powerful but practical, life-giving, Christ-exalting book. Let Nancy show you the way into a deeper love-relationship with your living, reigning redeemer that will change you forever.

—David Bryant, Founder, ChristNow.com
Author, *Christ Is NOW!*

*The Book **He Knows You by Name** Is a true reflection of who Nancy Wilson is! This faith filled Woman of God has written several books but this one stands out! Through this book, you will be inspired by Nancy's passionate life of evangelism and true demonstration of selfless love and compassion to fulfill the great commission. Have you ever wondered how you could connect individual felt needs with scriptural stories that in return encourage the heart to transform the mind? Look no more! **He Knows You by Name** is the key to unlock the mystery of evangelism!*

—Elisha Fredrick O. Abok, Pastor, Life & Leadership
Coach, Speaker, Leadership
Life Ministry Kenya

In a time where a generation is searching for significance, Nancy brings clarity to the truth of how God sees us and loves us as His precious children. Through personal stories and scriptures she emphasizes how specifically God knows us. She brings a timeless message to the forefront of one of the greatest giants facing our generation today: identity.

This book is more than a reflection of how God knows us by name, it is an invitation into the fullness of our identity – the dance of knowing God and being known by Him.

—**Niko Peele**, Founder & Director
Ignite Movement

Marcia and I have known Nancy as a dear friend for many years. **He Knows You by Name** *goes to the heart of Nancy's wanting to assure us of the deep love the Father and Son have for us. By sharing stories of the way Jesus related to those in need, Nancy uses Scripture, her personal encounters with others, and her poems to tell the story of His deep love for us and His desire to have a personal relationship with us. Nancy draws us to desire to have a much deeper relationship with our Savior like the one she has found.*

—**Ron Pershall**, President, Action-Impact
Pastor, East Nantmeal Christian
President, Viking Food Group

He Knows You by Name

God invites you into His eternal love story!

Nancy M. Wilson

He Knows You by Name
God invites you into His eternal love story!

Copyright © 2020 Nancy M. Wilson
ISBN: 978-1-949297-34-8
LCCN: 2020911424

Unless otherwise noted, all scriptures are from THE HOLY BIBLE NEW INTERNATIONAL VERSION®. Copyright© 1973, 1978, 1984, 2011 by Biblica, Inc.™. Used by permission of Zondervan.

Scripture quotations marked (NKJV) are taken from the NEW KING JAMES VERSION®, Copyright© 1982 by Thomas Nelson, Inc. Used by permission. All rights reserved.

Scripture quotations marked (NLT) are taken from THE HOLY BIBLE, NEW LIVING TRANSLATION, Copyright© 1996, 2004, 2007 by Tyndale House Foundation. Used by permission of Tyndale House Publishers, Inc., Carol Stream, Illinois 60188. All rights reserved. Used by permission.

Design and production by Diane A. Moore
Cover Design by Terri Oesterreich

Address all personal correspondence to:
Nancy M. Wilson
100 Lake Hart Drive, Dept. 1100, Orlando, FL 32832
Phone: (407) 443-7720
Email: *nancy.wilson@cru.org*
Website: *www.nancywilson.org*

Individuals and church groups may order books from Nancy Wilson directly, or from the publisher. Retailers and wholesalers should order from our distributors. Refer to the Deeper Revelation Books website for distribution information, as well as an online catalog of all our books.

Published by:
Deeper Revelation Books
Revealing "the deep things of God" (1 Cor. 2:10)
P.O. Box 4260
Cleveland, TN 37320
Phone: 423-478-2843
Website: *www.deeperrevelationbooks.org*
Email: *info@deeperrevelationbooks.org*

Deeper Revelation Books assists Christian authors in publishing and distributing their books. Final responsibility for design, content, permissions, editorial accuracy, and doctrinal views, either expressed or implied, belongs to the author.

Printed in the United States of America

Fear not
for *I have*
REDEEMED
YOU
I have *Called You*
by name:
You are MINE
...you are Precious
and honored
in My Sight
...because
I LOVE YOU
Isaiah 43:1b; 4 (NKJV)

Dedication

I dedicate this book to Jesus, my Beloved Savior and King, my Good Shepherd, who calls us each by name and leads us in His path and purpose for our lives. Who, but He, seeks each one of us so personally and passionately? I offer these true stories of His tender love, leading and miracle healing.

I will sing of the Lord's great love forever;
with my mouth I will make your faithfulness
known through all generations.
(Psalm 89:1)

And to all those who are seeking and searching...May you encounter the love of Our Shepherd, Savior and soon coming King!

My prayer for you, my friend...

How I long for you to grow more certain in your knowledge and more sure in your grasp of God himself. May your spiritual experience become richer as you see more and more fully God's great secret, Christ Himself! For it is in Him alone, that you will find all the treasures of wisdom and knowledge....it is in Jesus that God gives a full and complete expression of Himself. (Inspired by Colossians 2)

May your life reflect Him as you, too, *"declare His glory among the nations, His marvelous deeds among all people."* (Psalm 96:3)

I am forever grateful for Jesus who pursued and purchased me as His own, revealing to me the glory of His Story!

With all my love and devotion to Him,

Nancy

Acknowledgements

Words can't begin to express my gratitude to the many beloved friends who have encouraged and prayed for me! My faithful ministry partners who sacrificially give to enable me to fulfill my call as His Global Ambassador. I thank you with all my heart. It is an honor and privilege to be entrusted with your gracious support and prayers. May King Jesus reward you as only He can.

Without special time away to pray and write, I could not have His inspiration. My heartfelt thanks to my precious Sisters at Canaan in the Desert who welcomed me with love and care. Other friends also opened their homes to me...Jon and Molly Raynor, Deborah Cusick, Nancy Lillenberg and Pam and Bill Mutz. What a gracious blessing each of you have been!

I'm forever grateful to my precious friend, Rosa Greenway, who generously gave her skill in typing, managing and praying for me. I love you so much my dear friend.

Many thanks to my talented editors, Nancy Lillenberg, Dave and Linda Marcy, Trish Carpenter and especially Marcia Pershall who skillfully completed the process!

My talented cover designer, Terri Oestereich, your gift of design is excellent and your heart is beautiful.

Finally, I am rejoicing with my treasured friend, graphic designer, Diane Moore, who worked diligently with me and the staff at Deeper Revelation Books to carry this project through to completion. Di, you are an amazing woman of God; it is a joy to work with you.

Above all, to Jesus the Star in each story and His Holy Spirit who led me in each divine encounter.

To God be all the glory for He is the author of every story and promises to bring them all to completion!

With love and awe of Him,
His Beloved Bride and Scribe,
Nancy

Table of Contents

Note: Italics indicate a poem

The Love of God Is Greater Far

The love of God is greater far
Than tongue or pen can ever tell,
It goes beyond the highest star
And reaches to the lowest hell.
The guilty pair, bowed down with care,
God gave His Son to win;
His erring child He reconciled
And pardoned from his sin.

O love of God, how rich and pure!
How measureless and strong!
It shall forevermore endure—
The saints' and angels' song.

When hoary time shall pass away,
And earthly thrones and kingdoms fall;
When men who here refuse to pray,
On rocks and hills and mountains call;
God's love, so sure, shall still endure,
All measureless and strong;
Redeeming grace to Adam's race—
The saints' and angels' song.

Could we with ink the ocean fill,
And were the skies of parchment made;
Were every stalk on earth a quill,
And every man a scribe by trade;
To write the love of God above
Would drain the ocean dry;
Nor could the scroll contain the whole,
Though stretched from sky to sky.

Lyrics by Frederick Martin Lehman
Words & Music 1923, Ren. 1951 by Hope Publishing Co.
Carol Stream, IL 60188.

Introduction

God invites you into His eternal love story!

My beloved friend,

Thank you for choosing to begin this journey with me... discovering the love of God in every encounter and event in our lives.

As this beautiful song describes,

> *The love of God is greater far*
> *Than tongue or pen can ever tell.*
> *It goes beyond the highest star*
> *And reaches to the lowest hell.*

We see how limited is our understanding of the magnitude and intimacy of our Creator God and Eternal Father!

My prayer is for you to embark on an adventure with me, to encounter the love of God in a deep and personal way. *I pray the eyes of your heart be enlightened in order that you may know the hope to which he has called you.* (Ephesians 1:18a) and may you experience the magnificence of God who created and knows you by name!

As you read the words of this glorious hymn penned in 1917 by Frederick M. Leyman, consider the truth that the passionate love of God is for you and each of us, His precious creation. This is the theme of ***He Knows You by Name***!

I believe the wonder of God loving us and desiring a relationship with us can radically change your life as it has mine. You won't beable to keep into yourself!

Sometimes He overwhelms me with his glory and love, as he did the other day as I walked on the beach praising him for his breathtaking creation!

He inspired me by giving me the words of the poem that appears on the next page.

Oceans of Love

*Sky's proclaim your majesty,
for all to see your creativity;*

*People created for purpose and love,
look around, and up above;*

*Waves of revelation make them wonder,
sometimes you answer with thunder!*

*Clouds carry your glory,
as you reveal your story;*

*Foams of forgiveness wash away,
day after day they display;*

*Oceans of love for each one,
through the victory Jesus won;*

*He became our true life saver,
dying to give us eternal favor;*

*Won't you look up and around,
as you listen to the sound;*

*Jesus is calling you by name,
you can never remain the same;*

*Open your heart to explore,
the coming King to adore!*

How precious and personal He is! I am praying that you will discover the One who loves you more than anyone else in the entire world, as He reveals Himself uniquely to you.

Warmly in His love, as you journey with me,

Nancy

What's in a Name?

N ames are fascinating! They have meaning and purpose. In fact, many children are named with a destiny to fulfill. We especially see this in the Bible. A name is given with care, and God says He know us by name! Just think, when God created man and woman in His own image, He immediately gave them a purpose.

> *Then God said, "Let us make mankind in our image,*
> *in our likeness, so that they may rule over the fish in the sea and*
> *the birds in the sky, over the livestock and all the wild animals,*
> *and over all the creatures that move along the ground."*
> *So God created mankind in his own image,*
> *in the image of God he created them;*
> *male and female he created them.*
> (Genesis 1:26-27)

Their first assignment was to rule over God's awesome creation. He then blessed them and told them to "Be fruitful and increase in number!"

The name Adam means "Formed of Earth" and "In God's Image." Adam was given the task of naming all the beasts, birds and every living creature. Can you imagine that God entrusted him with a huge part of His creative work!

Smile... God already had a plan and purpose in mind. He put Adam into a deep sleep while He created and formed a woman from the rib He had taken from Adam. God graciously brought this crafted partner to Adam, and the man said,

> *"This is now bone of my bones and flesh of my flesh;*
> *she shall be called 'woman,' for she was taken out of man.*
> *That is why a man leaves his father and mother and*
> *is united to his wife, and they become one flesh."*
> (Genesis 2:23-24)

Eve's name means "Mother of Life"!

So from the very beginning of creation we see that God gives us names with our inherent purpose and destiny and then entrusts us to name what He gives to us!

We see this privilege most clearly in the naming of children. It amazes me how biblical characters are named with their purpose in mind.

Abraham means "Father of the Nations," David means "Beloved" and came to be called "A man after God's own heart!"

Isaiah means "God is my salvation" and his prophecies all involve the coming of the Promised Savior/Messiah!

It's really a fun discovery to learn about the meaning of names in the Bible and in our lives now.

My dear friend Pam prayed over each child in her womb, asking God what biblical figure she should pray they emulate in their character. One was the heart of David, the other was the devotion and courage of Daniel and one was the heart of Esther to stand up for such a time as this. Her naming was a big job, since she and Bill had twelve children and continue to pray into their destinies along with their grandchildren! God gives us our name with intentional purpose since He created us with a destiny.

I'll never forget my first experience speaking at a big youth conference in Nairobi, Kenya. Friendly new faces quickly became friends as they swarmed around me, introducing themselves. One by one they told me their unique and beautiful names, followed by... and this is what it means.

For example, Tabitha means "Gazelle" and implies "graceful."

George means "land worker" and the spiritual connotation is "walks with God."

Kaela means "cherished" and the spiritual connotation is "adored" from the Song of Solomon 6:3, *I am my beloved's and my beloved is mine.*

They didn't all tell me the spiritual connotation; I discovered that later. But can you imagine being a young guy named Hamil, which means "handsome" and the spiritual connotation is "Image of Christ." What a name to live up to!

As the conference continued, my new friends decided to give

me an African name. After much deliberation, they gave me my new name, "Tumaini," which means "Hope."

Needless to say, I was honored and blessed to be given this name and took it as my heart's passion to be a "bringer of hope" to these precious young African leaders.

A name can inspire us to live up to our destiny. It is a reminder of our individuality – that we are each uniquely made in the image of God! *God knows each one of us by name.* Because each of us is a special creation of God, our name is an integral part of who we are. God revealed this individuality to me in a very personal way.

One day I was studying the Bible and came to the book of Isaiah, Chapter 43. It's as if the words were written to me personally.

> *But now, this is what the Lord says—*
> *he who created you, Jacob,*
> *he who formed you, Israel:*
> *"Do not fear, for I have redeemed you;*
> *I have summoned you by name; you are mine.*
> *When you pass through the waters,*
> *I will be with you;*
> *and when you pass through the rivers,*
> *they will not sweep over you.*
> *When you walk through the fire,*
> *you will not be burned;*
> *the flames will not set you ablaze."*
> (Isaiah 43:1-2)

Let me explain...I was asking God to show me His plan and purpose for my life as a young twenty-one-year old.

I had known about how God chose Abraham to form a nation from whom the Messiah would come. But this was a fresh revelation that the covenant made with Abraham applies to all mankind who put their trust in Him (Exodus 3:14-15). In other words, I was now a part of this covenant promise; and the same intimate care He showed to the nation of Israel, He shows to all who follow Him.

We are grafted into these promises by faith in Yeshua (the

Hebrew name for Jesus), the Messiah, who came for all people from every tribe, tongue and nation. He is no respecter of people, He loves each one, as a Father loves His children.

"For God so loved the world that
he gave his one and only Son,
that whoever believes in him shall not perish
but have eternal life."
(John 3:16)

As I have grown in my understanding of the Bible, it has been such a joy to see His intimate, personal care for each of us.

"See, I have engraved you on the palms of my hands;
your walls are ever before me."
(Isaiah 49:16)

For you created my inmost being;
you knit me together in my mother's womb.
I praise you because I am fearfully and
wonderfully made;
your works are wonderful, I know that full well.
My frame was not hidden from you
when I was made in the secret place,
when I was woven together in the depths of the earth.
Your eyes saw my unformed body;
all the days ordained for me were written in your book
before one of them came to be.
(Psalm 139:13-16)

How precious to me are your thoughts, God!
How vast is the sum of them!
Were I to count them,
they would outnumber the grains of sand—
when I awake, I am still with You.
(Psalm 139:17-18)

As we move on to the New Testament, Jesus (Yeshua) was born, and throughout His time on earth, He showed us our Father's intimate love and care for each precious creation of His.

Not only this, but in the last book in the Bible, in Revelation 2:17, He tells His children that He will give us *a new name that no one knows except the one who receives it.* I can't wait to receive my new name for all eternity! Actually, I'd like to wait a bit longer; and until then, I want to invite you on a journey with me.

Just as my young African friends delighted in my knowing them by name, so each one of us desires to be known and loved for who we are. What a gift to be known and accepted without any condition of having "it all together!" In fact, how much more comforting is it to know that someone loves us unconditionally and believes in all we can become!

though *our* feelings come and go God's love does not.

Beautiful Are You

This love story began before the creation of the world when He chose us to be adopted as His sons and daughters through Jesus Christ (Ephesians 1:3-10). Then, in the secret place of your mother's womb you were knit together fearfully and wonderfully! (Psalm 139:13-16).

Your design was made by the One who fashioned and formed you for His delight and pleasure. Every day of your life was ordained and written in His book before one of them came to be.

How precious is this revelation to your soul! For this is only the beginning of a love pursuing you and personally planning your destiny for all eternity. Discovering the covenant of love the Lord had with Israel and how that extended to all of those who believed in the same God of Abraham, Isaac and Jacob was life changing for me.

The Song of Songs is a story of the love between King Solomon and the Shulamite maiden he falls in love with and pursues as his bride.

She experiences his love and responds...

> *Let him kiss me with the kisses of his mouth—*
> *for your love is more delightful than wine.*
> *Pleasing is the fragrance of your perfumes;*
> *your name is like perfume poured out.*
> *No wonder the young women love you!*
> *Take me away with you—let us hurry!*
> *Let the king bring me into his chambers.*
> (Song of Songs 1:2-4)

Later in the New Testament we see a beautiful description of Jesus Christ as He was poured out for us.

> *Not looking to your own interests but each of you*
> *to the interests of the others.*
> *In your relationships with one another,*
> *have the same mind-set as Christ Jesus:*
> *Who, being in very nature God, did not consider equality*

with God something to be used to his own advantage;
rather, he made himself nothing by taking the very nature
of a servant, being made in human likeness.
And being found in appearance as a man,
he humbled himself by becoming obedient to death—
even death on a cross!
Therefore God exalted him to the highest place
and gave him the name that is above every name,
that at the name of Jesus every knee should bow,
in heaven and on earth and under the earth,
and every tongue acknowledge that Jesus Christ is Lord,
to the glory of God the Father.
(Philippians 2:4-11)

He knows you by name; do you know Him by name?

What an eye opening experience it was for me when I discovered the intimate knowledge and care God had for me! I could not imagine that the God who created me would come to earth to pay our debt of sin and purchase our salvation with His own blood! But now this is what the Lord says,

He who created you O Jacob, He who formed you, O Israel:
"Do not fear, for I have redeemed you;
I have summoned you by name; you are mine."
(Isaiah 43:1)

"For I am the Lord your God,
the Holy One of Israel, your Savior."
(Isaiah 43:3)

It rocked my heart and captured me. Not only did He know me intimately but loved and accepted me in my imperfect, flawed condition.

I began to identify with the Shulamite maiden in the Song of Songs who was loved by the King,

You are altogether beautiful you are, my darling;
there is no flaw in you.
(Song of Songs 4:7)

You have stolen my heart, my sister, my bride;
you have stolen my heart
with one glance of your eyes,
with one jewel of your necklace.
(Song of Songs 4:9)

The king has been captivated by this maiden who becomes His bride. As love progresses, she finds her identity secure in his love.

I belong to my lover, and his desire is for me.
(Song of Songs 7:10)

And her passion grows with a longing to be set apart for him!

Place me like a seal over your heart,
like a seal on your arm; for love is as strong as death,
its jealousy unyielding as the grave.
It burns like blazing fire, like a mighty flame.
*(*Song of Songs 8:6)

This fiery bridal love consumes all lesser desires, by the wonder of being loved so completely and unconditionally. It truly is a love far greater than any other.

I invite you to a journey of discovery. As you experience Jesus encountering individuals, let Him meet you where you are, to touch your heart, your mind and just maybe change your life.

For He Knows You by Name and even sings a song over you.

The Lord your God is with you,
the Mighty Warrior who saves.
He will take great delight in you;
in his love he will no longer rebuke you,
but will rejoice over you with singing.
(Zephaniah 3:17)

I Know You by Name

Is it possible to be known?
An answer waiting to be shown.

Hungry hearts seeking care,
Someone to know and share;

All that is secret and dear,
Hidden sometimes by fear;

Ah, but there is One,
God's beautiful Son;

He came to reveal and heal,
No need for you to conceal,

Our deepest pain and loss,
He took for us on the cross.

Listen as He calls you by name,
You will never be the same!

He Knows You by Name

God invites you into His eternal love story!

Created and Designed by God

Walking the beach at sunset is a time of celebrating God's awesome work of creation. I considered the wonder and magnificence of His divine beauty and order created for us to enjoy. Rehearsing the story of creation from Genesis 1, I was struck anew with His grand design.

Not only did our Creator God exquisitely craft the universe we live in, but He fashioned each one of us in His own image, male and female.

Pondering this true account from the Bible, I watched the sun fade into the horizon. As the day darkened, I noticed a woman wading at the end of the ocean seemingly lost in her thoughts. I felt compassion for her; thinking she was troubled about something.

"How are you?" I asked. "I am clearing my mind. I needed to get away to think," she responded. I asked her name. "Donna," she replied.

I understand God's creation can help put life in perspective. I asked if she would like to hear a story. She looked curious as she nodded yes, I began to tell her the story of God's creation of the world from Genesis 1.

"Donna, what do you think about this story?" She began to open up to me about her life and her confusion. She had lost her job and her way in life and was searching for direction.

I assured her of God's personal love for her and that just as He intricately designed the world we live in, she was also His special creation. She lit up a cigarette and listened as I told her more of God's love for her through sending His Son, Jesus to pay for our sins and separation from Him. Seeing her distress, I asked if I could pray for her to discover His love and plan for her life. She nodded.

"Father, You love Donna. You see her confusion and struggle. You know her by name and care for her. Lead her and guide her. May she open her heart to receive Your Son, Jesus, and experience a personal relationship with You by simply asking and expressing her need for You."

As I looked up, she was crying. She then said that she had to go because her "honey" (her fiancé who also had lost his job) was coming.

Assuring her that I would continue to pray for her and him, I said goodbye and walked on carrying Donna in my heart and prayers, knowing that indeed the Lord "knows her by name" and is pursuing her heart.

Personal Reflection

Read the story of creation found in Genesis 1-2.

Reflect on God's intentionality in His physical creation of the world and His creation of man and woman.

Respond by praising Him for His name Elohim, Creator. *The heavens declare the glory of God; the skies proclaim the work of his hands.* (Psalm 19:1)

how cool that the same
God *who created*
mountains and oceans
looked *at you* *and galaxies*
and thought the *world* *needed*
one *of you, too!*

Wonder of It All

Who could ever imagine,
From where I did begin;

Jesus captured my heart,
Right from the very start;

I had to tell His Story.
To share His awesome glory!

What privilege is mine,
Lifting Jesus to shine;

Called to reconcile,
Sinners in exile;

For though our God is holy,
He gave His one and only;

Jesus suffered and died,
So we need not hide;

Grace and mercy revealed,
So we can be healed!

Passionately I proclaim,
There is no other Name!

Given to men for salvation,
Cause for joyous celebration!

Join me in this quest,
To reach all the rest!

For many stand in need,
To be forever freed,

From sin's eternal judgement,
Brought in to the Wedding Banquet!

Bow to Stand

Have you ever seen someone bent over and you felt their pain? Watching a man walk on the beach hunched over made me wonder if every step hurt him.

Well, I had heard an amazing story, as well as had one of my own, concerning a healed back; so spontaneously I shouted, "Are you okay?"

He came over to explain his plight, showing me the scars from his operation on his back.

"Wow, you look as if you are in pain; and I was feeling for you since I had fractured my back at one time in a trampoline accident."

He asked me to tell him what happened. I told him about my double back flip attempt while a camp counselor in college that resulted in a fall that left me temporarily paralyzed until I called out, "Jesus, help me." He was all ears.

The story continued with my miraculous recovery and no operation, only swimming and walking. I told him that Jesus cared for him, too, and I had another story I wanted to tell him. He listened as I began…

On a Sabbath Jesus was teaching in one of the synagogues, and a woman was there who had been crippled by a spirit for eighteen years. She was bent over and could not straighten up at all. When Jesus saw her, he called her forward and said to her, "Woman, you are set free from your infirmity." Then he put his hands on her, and immediately she straightened up and praised God. Indignant because Jesus had healed on the Sabbath, the synagogue leader said to the people, "There are six days for work. So come and be healed on those days, not on the Sabbath." The Lord answered him, "You hypocrites! Doesn't each of you on the Sabbath untie your ox or donkey from the stall and lead it out to give it water? Then should not this woman, a daughter of Abraham, whom Satan has kept bound for eighteen long years, be set free on the Sabbath day from what bound her?" (Luke 13:10-16)

So I asked Mike what he thought of the story. He was obviously touched by the way Jesus healed this dear woman. He didn't know much about Jesus' personal love; and though he went to church, he needed to be sure he was really trusting in Jesus to save him from his sins and painful condition. So Mike and I talked about how the Lord could help him.

After hearing more of my story, he went on his way considering what I had shared. "After all," I told him, "Jesus knows you by name and is the One who prompted me to call out to you. He knows and cares."

I am praying that Mike will bow his knee to God so that he can one day stand before Him totally healed.

Personal Reflection

Read Matthew 4:23-25 to understand Jesus' heart to preach the good news of the Kingdom and heal every disease and sickness among the people.

Reflect on Jesus' heart for this woman and each person suffering in any way. Imagine the contrast between Jesus and the religious leaders who were indignant because He healed on the Sabbath. What do you think caused them to begrudge her healing?

Respond by asking Jesus about any need in your life, whether it be healing your heart or body. Invite Him to lead you to reach out to others suffering physically and emotionally.

Let God be your guide.

You Are My Refuge

Today, Your mercies are new.
As I come to seek You.

You are my portion and cup,
As I lift my eyes to look up.

My home is in You alone.
May your glory be shown.

I will praise You, my King,
Who makes my heart sing.

What do I have to fear,
When El Shaddai is here;

Your holy presence is near,
Draws me to incline my ear;

Where can I go from Your presence,
Author of my very essence!

Entrusting my today and tomorrow,
Embracing joy and sorrow;

Trusting You hold my future,
In this, I am resting secure.

Praising You, who counsels me,
Setting my heart and soul free.

Because with You I am seated,
And cannot be defeated.

Therefore my heart is glad,
And cannot be sad.

My portion and joy forever,
Nothing can ever sever;

Delighting in Your glory,
What an awesome story!

Simon Peter Goes Fishing

D o you know about the greatest fisherman who ever lived? I asked with a light-hearted twinkle, as I stopped my walk on the beach. A father and daughter fishing duo looked at me with curiosity. I launched into the story...

Picture with me, by the Sea of Galilee, people crowding around Jesus to listen to Him. Jesus saw two boats at the water's edge left there by the fishermen who were washing their nets. He got into one of the boats belonging to Simon and asked him to put out a little from shore so He could sit down and teach the people. He then said to Simon, "Put out into the deep water and let down the nets for a catch."

Simon answered, "Master, we've worked hard all night and haven't caught anything. But because You say so, I will let down the nets."

They caught so many fish that their nets began to break. So they called their partners James and John, in the other boat, to come help. When Simon Peter saw this, he fell at Jesus' feet and said "Go away from me, Lord, I am a sinful man."

Then Jesus said to Simon, "Don't be afraid; from now on you will catch men." So they pulled their boats up on shore, left everything and followed Him.

Brianna loved hearing the story. As she watched her dad strain to bring the fishing line in...something was caught...it required all their effort to pull it in. Crowds had gathered around them to see what it would be. Then it happened...a big scary hammerhead shark was finally pulled in twisting and fighting with all its strength to get free.

Together they worked side by side until the rope was fastened over its mouth and teeth. Then, the hook was removed for all to see; and amazingly the shark was set FREE!

What an experience to watch as the father and daughter team worked to catch a shark. I smiled thinking of how I used to love doing things with my dad and how it pictures what Jesus taught.

"The Son can do nothing by himself; he can only do what he sees his Father doing, because whatever the Father does, the Son also does. For the Father loves the Son and shows him all he does." (John 5:19-20)

Why try to do anything without Our Father? He strengthens, leads and accomplishes all He invites us to do with Him, and how exciting it is when we fish for lost people with Him. We just may pull in a shark, destined to die, only to be set free.

Swimming in the ocean the next day, Brianna and her sister Ashley called me to show me the sand dollars they had found. After getting to know them better, I shared with them how I found Jesus as my truest treasure. They were both curious and interested but not yet ready to grasp His grace. They are still on the line thinking about this relationship with Jesus. As we said good-bye, I promised to pray for them that they would make the most important decision of their lives to receive Jesus as their Savior. Sometimes our job is just to hook their heart to seek the truth.

"Fishing with Jesus is an adventure! Cast your nets where He says, and expect Him to amaze you!"

Personal Reflection

Read Luke 5:1-10 and try to imagine the disciples' amazement at the catch of fish. Put yourself in the story as you read it.

Reflect on Peter's response. He and his companions were suddenly aware of Jesus' power to do anything and to know everything. It caused Peter to see his own sinful condition in the presence of Jesus.

Respond by asking yourself if Jesus has ever amazed you and then asked you to think of your life in light of who He is. Consider what He may be calling you to leave behind to follow Him.

Free to Soar

Lord Jesus, I want to fly,
Soaring in the sky!

Above all chaos and cares,
As I bring my desperate prayers;

Seeing the journey ahead,
Can make my heart dread;

Climbing rugged terrain,
Persevering with some pain;

I need you to be my guide,
Walking each step beside;

Knowing my unique stride,
You whisper, "Simply abide"

Letting go of all my fear,
And all I hold dear;

I take your hand and go,
To let the world know;

Such beauty and awe to see,
As I embrace my destiny...

Soaring with my King,
Makes my heart sing.

Leaps of faith are fun,
When you trust the SON.

Jesus is beyond compare,
Why not take His holy dare?

A Story in a Story

My plans to meet friends fell through, so before I could reset my day, I heard a familiar voice…

"Come away with Me my Beloved…"

An invitation from my beloved Lord, Savior and King was too precious to pass up. With an 80 degree forecast, the beach was calling my name. Savoring a special time with my Father and Friend, I walked the beach praying and praising Him!

"Lord Jesus," I prayed, "If You have anyone I am to share Your love with, show me."

It wasn't five minutes later when a couple came walking alongside me. I found out Ed and Ellen were from Washington, D.C. He worked in the government and she in Homeland Security. After thanking them for their service, I told them about my recent trip to Israel and how God was working there in spite of the challenges.

"One day, while in Israel," I shared, "my friends and I visited a Muslim village and were invited into a home to have coffee. Our gracious host and his seven brothers showed such hospitality. They told us they came from Iraq to settle in Israel because they wanted peace, so they built their village around a spring of fresh water. Tibeh is the name of the village, and it means "living water." We loved learning about their background, which led them to ask about us.

I shared a story that reminded me of their village that meant "living water" and also described my life. The seven men, along with my friends, listened closely as I told the story of Jesus' encounter with a woman at a well in Samaria where He offered her living water. (John 4) Through a translator, they seemed to understand the story with great interest and then told us they liked it a lot. They observed that Jesus really cared about the woman. Hearing the story seemed to open their hearts to experience Jesus' love.

It was a natural response for me to share how I identified with this woman as I searched for satisfaction in relationships, success, religion, etc. However, only when I received the grace, forgiveness and love of Jesus could my thirst be satisfied.

As I was telling Ed and Ellen what happened in the village of Nazareth, they understood Jesus' love and grace. Because they were curious to discover more, I shared how I had asked Jesus to show me Himself...who He was and how I could know Him.

Listening with interest, I gave them a copy of my own story to explain a little more about how they could know God personally. They thanked me warmly, expressing a desire to further investigate.

Back to Nazareth...Our new Muslim friends invited us to come back to their home to share more stories. Their unique story is still being written because he knows each one of us by name.

Personal Reflection

Read John 4:1-42 and observe how Jesus treated this woman. Consider the culture of that time. Jews and Samaritans didn't get along. Men did not regard women as equals but more as property.

Reflect on your own life. Have you ever searched for satisfaction in different places and still felt empty? What do you think the living water is referring to? Have you tasted the life-giving water Jesus offered her?

Respond if you have personally encountered Jesus' unconditional love and grace. Have you ever shared your story? The woman ran back to the village to tell everyone she met. Ask Him today to use your own story to touch someone else.

If you are still searching, you can encounter Jesus today, right where you are in your journey...take a drink from His limitless grace. He Knows You by Name!

Grace Overflowing

Grace flows from His throne,
That His love may be shown;

Grace given at such a cost,
Jesus, (my Beloved), died for the lost;

Grace came to set us free,
That the world may see;

Abba's heart beyond compare,
Grace flows through us to share.

Grace, immeasurably more,
Causes us to bow and adore!

true *peace* comes from knowing that *God* is in control.

Adopted by Abba

Kenya and Uganda, known as the "Pearl" of Africa, was my first major mission to Africa. Wow, was I excited! I knew God had called me to go to Africa ever since I was a young girl. But it wasn't until I was 19 years old that I discovered the life transforming destiny of knowing Jesus Christ personally. He then began to bring to reality the dreams and visions for which He had created me.

The adventure began as I embraced His heart and vision for the world. Along with that, my passion was to mobilize the next generation of young world changers. God opened the doors to entire high schools where we presented programs and shared the Gospel (Good News of Jesus). The spiritual hunger and need overwhelmed me with joy and sadness.

You see, in one school, Pearl High School, eighty percent of those who attend were orphans, who were in desperate need. My heart broke when I spoke about the *Pearl of Great Price, Jesus,* and I invited them to know their perfect heavenly Father through Jesus. They all responded with such simple childlike faith, hungry for the Father's love. Interacting with them after the program left our team with a huge awareness of need and hearts wanting to help.

"Lord," I prayed later that evening, "how can we possibly help all these precious young orphans? There are so many." Tears came to my eyes. Through His Word, He reminded me that He knows each of them by name. It's as if He spoke tenderly to me, whispering, "I love them more than you can imagine. You cannot care for all, but I will bring to you the ones you are to help."

He showed me so many promises about how He cares for the poor and the orphan. He is *a father to the fatherless, a defender of widows, is God in his holy dwelling.* (Psalm 68:5) He stoops down from heaven to look, and *He raises the poor from the dust and lifts the needy from the ash heap; he seats them with princes, with the princes of his people.* (Psalm 113:7-8)

"Yes, Lord, I will trust You to guide me."

Little did I know, the next day, He would lead me to a precious young woman named Sarah. Sarah shared her story with me: her parents had both died from AIDS when she was very young. Having no sense of belonging, she got pregnant in high school. She then went to live with an older man who promised to take care of her, but she soon realized after having a second child with him that he was not a good man. He began to abuse her first daughter Sheeba, and Sarah felt helpless and stuck with no place to go.

Immediately, I began thinking of how she could find a way out, but I came to see how impossible it was for her.

Through my tears, I told her, "Sarah, only God knows how to help you! I want to introduce you to your Perfect Father, Abba God who loves and cares for you dearly."

As I shared the Gospel with Sarah, her heart was touched to respond and receive Jesus Christ as her Savior.

We were both so happy that we cried tears of joy. Even so, the situation remained the same. I told her we should both pray that evening and ask Our Father what to do.

The next day, Sarah informed me that she knew she must send Sheeba to boarding school where the man could not hurt her; but she had no money. It was so clear to me that day that Sarah was one of the "ones" I was called to help. I had just enough to send Sheeba to school for the first semester, so I gave her the money by faith. When I returned home, I discovered that a church had sent a gift to me that very day with the exact amount.

This experience changed me forever, allowing me to trust God that my little loaves and fishes would be multiplied as He leads! Sarah was "the one God had brought into my life to help" that day. Praise God! Sheeba received Jesus as her Savior and is now thriving in college. Sarah has started a beauty supply business, which is special to me because my dad began a beauty supply business many years earlier. He was an example to me in caring about the poor and underprivileged,

Jesus knows and cares about each precious child in the entire world, no matter the situation. He knows each of us by name and has inscribed us on the palms of His hands.

"Can a mother forget the baby at her breast and
have no compassion for the child she has borne?
Though she may forget, I will not forget you!
See, I have engraved you on the palms of my hands;
your walls are ever before me."
(Isaiah 49:15-16)

Personal Reflection

Read Ephesians 1:3-6 and observe the words *chosen blameless* and *adopted*.

Reflect on the revelation of God as our Abba Father who desires to adopt each one into His eternal family!

The Spirit you received does not make you slaves,
so that you live in fear again; rather, the Spirit you
received brought about your adoption to sonship.
And by him we cry "Abba, Father." The Spirit himself
testifies with our spirit that we are God's children.
Now if we are children, then we are heirs—heirs of
God and co-heirs with Christ, if indeed we
share in His sufferings in order that
we may also share in his glory.
(Romans 8:15-17)

Respond by receiving a fresh revelation of our Heavenly Father's love and pursuit of you. Ask Him to fill those broken places in your heart with His perfect fatherly love for you. He Knows You by Name!

Precious Abba

My soul cry's out,
with a joyous shout.
Abba, Daddy so great.
On You I will wait.

Tears of gratitude flow,
My love I want to show;

What glory on display,
No words can ever say;

Beyond my comprehension,
Is heaven's full dimension.

Now to be here on earth,
Inviting people to rebirth.

The whole world must know,
What Jesus' cross did show.

Sins forgiven, price paid,
On Him all sin was laid.

"It is finished!" He cried.
Abba must have a sighed.

Such a great cost,
So no soul would be lost;

Victorious battle fought,
So you could be bought.

Three days later He arose,
Now His Deity shows.

Jesus conquered the grave,
So you can be saved.

Come eternal life to receive,
No more need to grieve.

Hallelujah to Our King,
May every heart Sing!

You are invited,
Love Abba

◦𝒜 𝒞hosen 𝒟estiny

Africa and the next generation of young leaders found a place deep in my soul. I know it was a divine call from God. I believe in them, love them and am blessed to invest in them through preaching, teaching and training. What a privilege to help lead many others to get involved also!

In 2004, I had the joy of ministering at a youth conference organized by LIFE Ministry. Leading training for youth leaders, I met an amazing young leader named James Kintu. His humble, loving and teachable spirit touched my heart. Immediately, I could see the Lord had given him a heart for the poor and the orphans. He also shared my passion to invest in the next generation of young leaders.

We stayed in touch as he would email me about his progress in reaching out to high school campuses in Uganda and mobilizing others to pray and share the Gospel! I could see God was growing a young leader equipped for His purposes!

One day, James emailed me sharing that God had clearly impressed upon him that it was now time for him to give back to the Lord all He had given to him.

Here are James' words:

While a long struggle with life challenges, for many years as a Christian since 1998, trying to do all types of work, the Lord called me and told me that I need you to care for orphans, reminding me that you were an orphan, that I helped you and educated you for this very purpose. Then I had to accept and follow the will of God before telling me to care for needy and orphans. He also told me to serve Him by evangelizing to the youth of this generation, something the Lord gave me with an assurance that He will fulfill and what He has called me to do.

My vision for Chosen Academy is to help these young and once desperate children of the Lord to grow up as responsible Christians not forgetting what the Lord has done for them. By using Mum Nancy and other loving friends to support them in education, we encourage them to grow up with the fear of the Lord in their lives. It is almost similar to the vision that my Mum Nancy has shared in her book, **Chosen With A Mission**. Likewise, I was chosen by the Lord for a mission of evangelizing to the youth and caring for the orphans; a work/calling that I do with love and compassion. The Lord has used Mum Nancy to show me a proper way of serving the Lord without reservations and with love while serving the Lord as though He is coming back today."

I'll never forget the day James took a bus to Kenya to meet me and share the vision God had put in his heart to begin a school for the poor and orphaned children! He asked me to be the "Patron Mother". The Lord quickened my heart to believe with James as I declared, "Son, your mother is a missionary who lives by faith, you have no money, but our Father in heaven owns everything! We will believe God together."

It's as we prayed for the name, the Lord impressed upon both of us with the name of my first book **Chosen With A Mission,** which captures God's heart for this generation.

Together with many beloved partners and friends we are believing God to raise up "world changers"! As of today we have 350 precious students along with a devoted team of teachers and workers. Praise God!

We give Him all the glory for what He has and continues to do. It is a privilege to be a part of carrying out our King's enterprises!

James is fulfilling the destiny God has created him for! His name means "Nurtured." Indeed he has been nurtured by the Good Shepherd Jesus. I'm so honored to be the "Patron Mother" of Chosen Academy, Indeed, the Lord fulfilled a promise He gave to me to have many spiritual children who would influence nations! (Isaiah 54:1-3)

My friend, Jesus knows you by name and has a good plan for your life. This promise has shaped my life and calling and that of my spiritual son James. What a miracle that He has intertwined our lives together in such a beautiful way!

49

"For I know the plans I have for you, declares the Lord,
plans to prosper you and not to harm you,
plans to give you hope and a future."
(Jeremiah 29:11)

May you also embrace this promise...for He Knows You by Name!

Personal Reflection

Read Psalm 113. Praise Him for His intimate care for the poor and needy,

Reflect on the Lord's awareness of every detail of your life and situation. How has He shown His care for you?

Respond by asking Him to reveal more of the purpose and plan He has created for you. Keep a journal of the dreams He places in your heart.

Just think –

You're not here by chance but God's choosing.
His hand formed you and made you
the person you are.
He compares you to no one else, you are one of a
kind. You lack nothing that
His grace can't give you.
He has allowed you to be here at this
time in history to fulfill His special
purpose for this generation.

By Roy Lessin

Show Me Your Way

*My Abba I pray,
each and everyday...*

*Show me Your way
that I may obey!*

*You are my light
in the midst of night.*

*Shine ever so bright
and lead me right.*

*You the potter, I the clay,
fashion me for Your way.*

*I will not go without you
who makes all things NEW!*

*So here I am my love,
soaring with your Holy Dove!*

stay *right,* *follow* *God's* path.

Ambassador on Assignment

The day arrived for my book signing! What an incredible, faith-filled journey it had been. Beginning with a desperate prayer, "Lord Jesus, please find a way that I can share the good news of who Jesus is in Turkey."

Knowing it was illegal to share with anyone under 18, my heart longed for these precious high school students to hear about Jesus. For a moment I thought of following in Apostle Paul's footsteps, after all, I have been nicknamed Paulette. Prison ministry might be fruitful. But better judgment stopped me in my tracks! What about the local believers I could put at risk?

My earnest prayers began. Every morning I prayed walking the city declaring (Isaiah 60:1-4), that the light and glory of God would rise in Turkey. Later in the week, a by-chance meeting with a radio host landed me an invitation to be a guest on his radio show. With gusto and faith I shared my personal testimony, which included the glorious message of Jesus' grace! People called in to ask about the books I had written in English and wanted to know if they were also in Turkish. The radio host assured them that they would be translated and published in Turkish. Wow, I realized that prayer had opened a new door; but I wondered how all this could happen.

He assured me it must be done. My faith journey continued, one miracle after another, finances, translation, publishing, until the day arrived for my first Turkish book signing. How excited and expectant I was. God had opened this door and I was told that the Turkish Book Fair was a big event in Istanbul, and I knew God had opened the door.

I woke up early that morning and went out for a jog. Then I decided to stop and enjoy the hotel's breakfast buffet. Placing my jacket on a chair, I went to choose from the scrumptious food. Returning to my table, I was surprised when a very dignified and well-dressed man was seated across from my place at the table. Feeling a bit embarrassed about wearing my jogging attire, I decided to simply enjoy a new acquaintance. As I introduced myself and asked his name, he said it was

"Mohammed." Asking where he was from and why he was there caused me to quickly lose interest in the food.

"I am the Ambassador from Iraq to Turkey!"

"Oh my, that is wonderful! I've been praying for Iraq and the soldiers," I told him.

"Why do you care so much about our nation?" he asked.

I swallowed hard, and said with sincerity, "I believe the Prince of Peace cares deeply about the people in Iraq; and I have come to know Isa, Jesus, the Prince of Peace in a personal, life-changing way."

His curiosity was peaked! "Tell me more about this."

In the next half hour, I shared God's eternal love, giving an overview of the Gospel from creation to His return. His interest prompted me to personalize my story of searching for truth and purpose. After studying various world religions, I realized religion wasn't the answer, but that God desires for us to have a personal relationship with Him. I came to discover God's love demonstrated by His sending His only Son Jesus to pay for our sins. As he listened intently, I explained how he could open His heart to receive Jesus as His Savior when the time came that he believed. He thanked me profusely, expressing deep gratitude because he had never heard anything like this before. He then asked me what I did and why I was in Turkey. To his surprise, I told him that I was there for the Book Fair with my new book in Turkish and that I, too, am an ambassador."

"For who? he asked."

"Not for just any king," I responded, "but for the King of ALL Kings!"

He smiled as if he understood. He thanked me for sharing my story with him and helping him to understand more of who Jesus is. We shook hands and said goodbye! I told him I would continue to pray for his nation and for him to come to know "The Prince of Peace."

After my divine encounter, I went to the Book Fair with joy. What a delight and honor it was for me to sign 200 books personally for young Muslim girls and to give many other books away.

Adventures await all "Ambassadors on Assignment," for their job is to represent the King.

Personal Reflection

Read 2 Corinthians 5:20-21.

Reflect on what it means to be an ambassador.
An ambassador:
- represents his country and his leader.
- delivers the King's message.

Respond by asking King Jesus to give you His heart to fulfill this calling.

On Spirit Wings

Embarking on a new adventure,
Privilege beyond measure;

Representing My Beloved King,
Makes my heart and soul sing;

Expecting to see Your glory,
As I tell Your love story;

Remaining in Your embrace,
Surrounded by Your grace;

Ministering angels all the way,
Spirit leading what to say;

Loving Abba goes before,
Opening every door;

Lifting high Jesus' Name,
Telling of His beauty & fame;

Praising Him for hearts to hear,
Of My Savior's love so dear;

Soaring on spirit wings ,
I will see brand new things!

ℳ Chosen Seat

T his seat is for you; it is better than the other location," the kind stewardess said. As I sat down, I was warmly greeted by Karina who was on her way to India. Her eagerness to talk opened an opportunity for me to tell her a story after I listened to hers.

Her marriage was arranged, but she was searching for more. As she shared her quest to explore various religions, I sensed a hunger in her to know God in an intimate way. Eagerly, she listened to the story of how Jesus had a friendship with Mary, Martha and their brother Lazarus.

Lazarus was sick and the sisters sent for Jesus. However, Jesus stayed away until Lazarus died and then He went to them. Mary and Martha were grieving and so disappointed that Jesus had not come sooner.

Jesus told Martha, *"Your brother will rise again."*

Martha said, *"I know he will rise again in the resurrection at the last day."*

Jesus said to her, *"I am the resurrection and the life. The one who believes in me will live, even though they die."* (John 11:25)

After seeing Mary weeping, along with others He was deeply moved in spirit and troubled. He went to where they had laid Lazarus and wept.

"See how he loved him," they said.

But some asked, *"Could not he who opened the eyes of the blind man have kept this man from dying?"*

Jesus, deeply moved, came to the tomb. *"Take away the stone,"* He told them.

"But Lord," Martha said, *"He has been there for four days."*

Then Jesus said, *"Did I not tell you that if you believed, you would see the glory of God?"*

So they took the stone away and Jesus looked up and said, *"Father I thank you that you have heard me, but I say this that the people standing here will believe that you sent me."*

Jesus then called in a loud voice, *"Lazarus come out!"*

The dead man came out, wrapped in linen.

Jesus said to them, *"Take off the grave clothes and let him go."* (John 11:44)

Karina told me she knew God had planned for me to sit next to her and that He had arranged for us to meet. She was touched by this miracle. After much discussion about who Jesus was, she said that He was like Krisna, one of the 330,000,000 gods Hindus believe in; the one she followed. This was all she had ever heard.

I sensed a curiosity in her and began to share my story of how I searched out His uniqueness as a 19-year-old college freshman while exploring all the world religions. I discovered God's heart to have a personal relationship with us.

Her interest led me to tell her another story in which Jesus forgives sins. Her openness gave me freedom to ask if I could pray for her to discover who Jesus is, the One who gave His life to save her from having to try hard enough to be forgiven of her sins!

We said goodbye with the promise of connecting again after her trip to India. I left Karina with the sweet fragrance of Jesus to savor. May her search be satisfied by the sweetest name I know… Jesus.

Personal Reflection

Read Romans 10:14, *How, then, can they call on the one they have not believed in? And how can they believe in the one of whom they have not heard? And how can they hear without someone preaching to them?*

Reflect on your journey to explore the claims of Jesus Christ and consider the difference between trying to "satisfy" the demands of God by earning His love versus "receiving" the forgiveness of our sins through Jesus who has power over sin and death!

Respond by inviting Jesus to reveal who He is to you and to those you may be praying for as He boldly declared, *"I am the resurrection and the life. The one who believes in me will live, even though they die; and whoever lives by believing in me will never die. Do you believe this?"* (John 11:25-26)

My Rescuer

What can I say, but to pray?
You meet me in every way!

I am longing as a deer,
For you to be near;

"Come to me, my child,
My love is free and wild!"

When I am down and out,
You raise a victory shout!

Released from fear,
Your Word, I hear!

Giving hope to my heart,
Embracing a new start;

I am held in your arms,
Shielded from life's harms;

Released from the grave,
You came to save!

Oh, for all to know,
Your miracles to show!

In awe of YOU,
Your Beloved Bride

A Love Story

S avoring the beauty of Switzerland, I made my way upward to the castle. As I watched the swans on the lake, there in front of me was a beautiful young Swiss woman. She too had stopped to admire the charming lake. This was her day off and being a young 21-year-old, she planned later to go shopping. Rachel was her name.

"Oh, Rachel, you are beautiful! I know a love story about another young woman named Rachel. Would you like to hear it?"

"Yes, she replied, smiling.

I began, "This is a true story from the Bible about a young man named Jacob who fell in love with beautiful Rachel. He agreed to work seven years for her hand in marriage and said they seemed like only a few days because of his love for her! But his uncle tricked him and after seven years of working for him, he gave his other daughter Leah to be Jacob's wife. Jacob loved Rachel so much that he worked another seven years for her."

Rachel seemed open to hear more.

I continued, "This is but a small picture of God's love for us. He was willing to send His Son Jesus to give His life to purchase us as His Bride for all eternity. Have you heard much about Jesus?" I asked.

Rachel only knew a little and was curious. Sharing how His love became real in my life at age 19 when I was trying to understand how God and Jesus intersected with my future, we connected. She agreed to read the Gospel of John and explore Jesus for herself! His pursuing love had already tugged at her heart. His love, like Jacob's, would go to any extent to win her for Himself.

I had the joy of introducing them. A forever love story!

Personal Reflection

Read the love story of Jacob and Rachel in Genesis 29:1-30.

Reflect on how the Bible relates to every human experience, whether joyful or painful. He pursues us with His love.

Respond by being more aware that the people we encounter every day have deep longings and needs that only Jesus can meet! He can use us to reach out with His love.

Beautiful You Are

Beloved body of Christ,
Purchased and prized;

Beautiful Shepherd King
Praises to proclaim and sing,

Beautiful promises to hold,
Declared and told;

Beautiful beloved bride,
Reigning at His side;

Beautiful feet to preach,
Many lost to reach;

Beautiful, no two the same,
He Knows You by Name.

ℐ 𝒦now 𝒴our 𝒫ain

I t was late. I had been traveling in Cameroon speaking in high schools throughout the village towns. What an amazing day of sharing the personal love of Jesus with these precious young students. Many had responded to His love and forgiveness. My heart was full, but my body was weary.

Checking into the remote hotel at 11:00 pm was a welcome treat. Morning would come soon, since I had been asked to speak to an entire high school assembly just as school began.

A sweet young woman named Pasquelina checked me into my room. As I prepared to say good night, I sensed a nudge from the Holy Spirit to engage more with her.

"Pasquelina, may I tell you a story?" I asked.

"Yes!" She smiled, "I'm not too busy, as you can see."

Jesus went to a town called Nain, and his disciples and a large crowd went along with him. As he approached the town gate, a dead person was being carried out— the only son of his mother, and she was a widow. A large crowd from the town was with her. When Jesus saw her, his heart went out to her and he said, "Don't cry."

Then he went up and touched the casket they were carrying him on and everyone stood still. He said, "Young man, I say to you, get up!" The dead man sat up and began to talk, and Jesus gave him back to his mother.

They were all the filled with awe and praised God. "A great prophet has appeared among us," they said. "God has come to help his people." This news about Jesus spread throughout Judea and the surrounding country. (Luke 7:11-17)

Her response to the story stunned me as her demeanor changed to sadness. "One of my children died," she quietly told me. My heart went out to her. I could see the pain and sadness in her eyes.

Unknowingly, I had told her about a mother whose son had died. Jesus had reached out with compassion and brought the boy back to life. How could this comfort her, I thought?

The Holy Spirit took over as He flooded me with love for

Pasquelina. Prompted by His care for her, I reached out and told her.

Just like Jesus saw this widow in her pain, He sees you and cares about you and your great loss.

"Do you know Jesus' personal love for you?" I gently asked.

"I don't know much about Him," she responded.

For the next fifteen minutes, I had the joy and privilege of sharing His tender love and grace with her. Pasquelina was ready to receive Jesus' gift of love and salvation! She understood that His great love had led Him to take our pain and sin upon Himself on the cross. He had met with her right where her heart's need was. That late night was right on time for Pasquelina!

Jesus also renewed my strength as I marveled once again at how He knows each one of us by name and can use us to share His name!

Personal Reflection

Read the story of this widow again in Luke 7:11-16. Imagine you are there in the crowd. What would you think? Let your heart take in Jesus' personal love, compassion and power over death.

Reflect in praise for who He is and how He cares for each individual. Thank him for caring for you in your pain, loss and hurt. Ask Him to meet you at your point of need.

Respond by personally inviting Jesus into your heart if you have never received His gift. Pray about reaching out to someone you know who is experiencing some loss or pain. Consider telling him or her this beautiful story.

The Lord is close to the brokenhearted
and saves those who are crushed in spirit.
(Psalm 34:18)

Treasures Of Darkness

Inspired by Isaiah 45

When we do not know the way,
In His presence, we must stay;

He alone knows you by name,
No two of us are the same;

Hidden wealth in secret places,
Fill up our empty spaces;

Adonai goes before you,
Taking you through;

Making crooked places straight,
Shattering heavy weight;

He cuts through iron bars,
Healing us, by His scars;

Hidden in your confusion and pain,
Lies deep revelation to gain;

Light of the world shines,
As He gently molds and refines;

He is the Holy One, your maker,
A faithful and skillful potter;

In His arms is perfect shalom,
His divine will, a secure home;

Why question and complain,
Your life, He does ordain;

Lift your eyes on high,
Commit your life to Adonai!

Crash Connection

Magnificent beach...gorgeous day...calling upon the Lord... walking on the beach in Abu Dhabi.

"Lead me Abba to your beloved 'covered' daughters," I prayed.

After an invigorating swim, I went to change before getting a taxi. There, in the changing room, was a woman entirely covered in black, yet a radiant smile when I greeted her. Her name was Egypt.

Marhaba (hello in Arabic) was all I knew how to say besides *Shukran* which is thank you and *Salaam* the word for peace. After using up my vocabulary, she extended her hand to me warmly. What an invitation for me to give her a gift! I offered her the DVD **Magdalena**, in Arabic, the story of Jesus through the eyes of Mary Magdalena. Smiling, she received it and we parted after a kiss on both cheeks. I pray I will meet her again in heaven.

Happily, I left to catch a cab home, when I discovered an accident had occurred. A van had run into a cab and they were waiting for the police. Looking at the van I saw a woman covered in black behind the wheel. Without hesitation I went to see if I could help her. Rolling down her window, I asked if she was okay. We then introduced ourselves. Her name was Ameena and although she was not injured, she seemed visibly shaken.

I assured her the damage could be fixed and I would help anyway I could as she waited for the police.

She got out of the car to inspect the damage it and I began to learn about her life. She was a young single woman who had three sisters and two brothers.

"Wow!" I told her, "I have four brothers and one sister."

We connected at a heart level and she said, You are so kind."

"I know what it feels like to be in an accident. It is my pleasure to help you in any way possible," I responded.

After the police came, Ameena offered to take me home. We talked and got to know each other. She wanted to come to the singles event I was speaking at that night, but due to the distance it would not work out.

I offered to stop by her work the next day before I left for Dubai. The next day I went to her office with chocolates for her and her family.

Ameena and I shared more about our lives and exchanged emails to keep in touch. Prayerfully I asked her if she would like to receive another gift. I brought her the DVD of **Magdalena** in Arabic.

She smiled and said, "Why not. Is this all about Isa (Arabic for Jesus)?"

"Yes," I responded, "and it shows His great love and honor of women." I shared one of the stories in the video with her about how Jesus (Isa) healed a precious woman who had been bleeding for twelve years. She courageously reached out and touched His robe and was instantly healed.

Jesus commended her in front of the crowd saying, *"Daughter your faith has healed you, go in peace."*

Ameena was touched by the story and said she was eager to watch the video with her mother and sisters.

Sharing more about my journey of getting to know Jesus in a personal way, she listened closely. I left assuring her of my prayers for God to bless her and her family and to provide a good husband for her.

She hugged me and thanked me saying, "Yes, I will wait for the right one."

I am praying she will first meet the Prince of Peace and become His Bride forever.

Thanks be to His divine connections as He crashed into the lives of His precious daughters.

Personal Reflection

Read Luke 8:1-56, taking note of Luke 8:43-48 (Jesus' encounter with the bleeding woman).

Reflect on the need many people have to experience the love of Jesus.

How can your prayers and preparation equip you to be His witness?

Knowing how to share the miracle stories of Jesus can prepare you to engage with people of all cultures and backgrounds.

Respond by praying for many precious people who are living in spiritual blindness, never having heard the truth about Jesus' gift of salvation.

Ask Jesus to use you to share His love and truth as you connect with their hearts. Pray specifically for family, friends and neighbors who need Him.

*And even if our gospel is veiled, it is veiled to those who are
perishing. The god of this age has blinded the minds of
unbelievers, so that they cannot see the light of the gospel
that displays the glory of Christ, who is the image of God.
For what we preach is not ourselves, but Jesus Christ as
Lord, and ourselves as your servants for Jesus' sake.
For God, who said, "Let light shine out of darkness,"
made his light shine in our hearts to give us the light of the
knowledge of God's glory displayed in the face of Christ.*

*But we have this treasure in jars of clay to show that this
all-surpassing power is from God and not from us.*
(2 Corinthians 4:3-7)

Poured Out Love

My Beloved, so pure and holy
Made Himself weak and lowly;

Surrendered His glory,
To begin a love story!

All creation under a curse.
He alone could reverse;

Purchase price so high,
Lamb of God had to die;

Cup of sufferings real,
Broken break as a seal,

Father turned away,
On that fateful day;

Jesus carried the weight of sin,
All our selfish pride within;

Every heartache, pain and loss,
He carried on the cross;

Covenant love in His blood,
Poured out as a flood,

Washing away the wall,
Every knee will one day fall;

King Jesus conquered and arose!
Everyone on earth knows,

Love so amazing, so divine.
Jesus, Savior, King is mine!

A "Magical" Experience

I mmersing myself in another culture has always been exciting to me. What could be better than staying in the home of my Ethiopian friends who lived in a predominantly Muslim village? I had been invited to speak at a youth conference in Ethiopia to train and equip high school students in outreach ministry. Their zeal and passion for Jesus and for their country was evident.

Every morning I would get up early and prayer walk/run the neighborhood I was staying in. One particular morning I was exercising at a small park area in the middle of the village. Suddenly, I noticed a young boy around 14 years old watching me with curiosity. Stopping to say hello, he introduced himself as Albert and his young brother as Mohammed. After getting to know a little about Albert, I invited him to join me as I walked and jogged around the park. He seemed so happy. Since it was Ramadan I asked if he were fasting—and he said that he was.

I told him I admired his desire to please God and know Him better. Then I asked if he would like to hear a true story from God's Word. He smiled eagerly so I began.

"One day as Jesus was passing through a city many people followed Him. There was a man named Zacchaeus, a very wealthy tax gatherer, curious about Jesus. But being too short to see, he ran ahead to climb a tree. When Jesus reached the spot He looked up and said,

"Zacchaeus, come down immediately I must
stay at your house today."
Zacchaeus welcomed him gladly, and all the people muttered.
"He has gone to be the guest of a sinner." But Zacchaeus stood
up and said to the Lord, "Look, Lord! Here and now I give half
of my possessions to the poor, and if I have cheated anybody out
of anything, I will pay back four times the amount."
Jesus said to him, "Today salvation has come to this house,
because this man, too, is a son of Abraham.
For the Son of Man came to seek and to save the lost."
(Luke 19:1-10)

Albert liked the story, so I asked him if he had ever thought about Jesus' knowing him by name? He hadn't, so I shared how much God loved him and had created him uniquely for a special purpose. I assured him that He wanted Albert to know Him in a personal way.

Albert listened intently so I continued by sharing my story about how I learned to know more of why Jesus came and how I opened my heart to ask Him into my life to pay for my sins. I asked him if he would like to watch a video that shared more stories of Jesus. Yes, he did! So he walked back with me to the home where I was staying and I gave him a **Jesus** DVD in Amharic, his language. I prayed for him that he might be touched by the message.

"Knock, knock!" The next morning Albert was there at my door, joined by a friend Yonas, who was the same age. He had the video in his hand and when I asked if he watched it, a big smile lit up his face.

"It was magical! Magical!" he exclaimed.

His friend had also watched it and they both said they had prayed to ask Jesus to come into their heart. Not being fully sure of what they understood, I invited them to the village church in a tent where I would be speaking that Sunday. They came and met some other youth who promised to keep in touch with them. Obviously, Jesus was drawing their hearts, but it would be a journey getting to know Him better. I had the joy of sowing seeds of love and truth that would be followed by others. One thing I do know:.. Jesus knows each heart and each name as He calls out

> *Yet to all who did receive him,*
> *to those who believed in his name,*
> *he gave the right to become children of God.*
> (John 1:12)

Have you heard Him call you by name? If so, are you sharing His love and truth with others? Pray for Jesus to lead you today to reach out to a neighbor, a friend or someone you meet.

Personal Reflection

Read the story of Zacchaeus in Luke 19:1-10 and think about what you see in this story that touches you. Can you relate to Zacchaeus in any way?

Reflect on the fact that Jesus knew Zacchaeus by name. and He Knows You by Name, as well as each person He created. What difference does that make in your life?

Respond by thanking Jesus for His personal, intimate care for each person. Ask Him how you can show that same kind of love to others without judgement, seeing them through His eyes of love and purpose.

Lift Up Your Eyes

Look up *into the sky,*
See Jesus who did die;
Though He died, He lives.
His Spirit to us He gives;
He is the pearl to treasure,
His worth beyond measure;

Look around, *Hear the sound,*
Time now for lost and found;
Give His wedding invitation,
Without fear or hesitation;
The King is inviting one and all,
Will you hear His holy call?

Look into *your own heart,*
Do you long for a new start?
Be prepared as His bride,
In His love to abide;
Soon He comes on the clouds,
All will bow, as the trumpet sounds!

Divine Exchange

hat is the exchange rate in dollars?" I asked the beautiful young attendant at the bank in Switzerland as she graciously helped me. I noticed her name was Emmadina and discovered she was from Albania. Thanking her for her help, I gave her a little inspiration card about prayer. She told me she was a Muslim and gladly received it.

"My friend Elvadina is a Muslim from Bosnia; I thought you might be also" I said. We have shared stories about Jesus, the One you know as the Prophet Isa. "Would you like to hear one?"

"Yes! I'm not busy. Please tell me."

Telling the story of Jesus' encounter with a woman who had been bleeding for twelve years, and was instantly healed when she reached out to touch Jesus' robe, touched her heart! She clearly saw Jesus' love when He said to the woman, *"Daughter, your faith has healed you, go in peace."*

Eager to hear another story, I told her about a woman who had a bad reputation and came to Jesus while He was eating at a religious leader's home. She came into the house weeping and knelt at His feet as she washed His feet with her tears and wiped them with her hair. She then anointed His feet with very expensive oil and began to kiss them. In spite of the negative reaction of the religious leaders, Jesus commended her for her love and forgave her sins.

Emmadina began to discuss with me how Jesus showed God's love. A window of her heart opened as I shared how Jesus came to forgive all of us through His death on the cross. Though not fully convinced of His deity, she listened as I shared my story of discovering how Jesus' death and resurrection could bring me new life now and the promise of eternal life forever! She agreed to read more in the Injeel (New Testament in Arabic) about Jesus, and what He Himself said.

A divine exchange took place that day at the bank, which is more valuable than anything you or I could buy; an investment for eternity.

Personal Reflection

Read the story about the bleeding woman and a dead girl who came to life found in Luke 8:40-56.

Also read the beautiful story of the forgiven woman who anointed Jesus in Luke 7:36-50.

Reflect on the many people of different faiths who don't know these true stories about Jesus that reveal God the Father's heart of compassion and love.

Respond in prayer for many who don't know anything about Jesus and ask Him to use you to share His life and love with those who need to hear.

Seeing Ahead

Climb every mountain...
Drink from His fountain!

Endless dreams ahead,
A new path to tread...

Never been this way,
I simply must obey!

"Shepherd, guide and King
I surrender everything;

Take my hand to lead,
Daily I will plead!

If you don't go with me,
My eyes cannot see...

Your vision is brand new;
Once again, I say, I do!"

"Like God"

Delighting in my successful climb to the top of a mountain peak in the Arizona desert, I spent some time giving glory and praise to God for His awesome creation.

Unaware of anyone else on the trail, I was singing and smiling as I descended the peak. Then I soon caught up with a fellow traveler named Michael.

"I saw you up there so full of life, lifting your hands up to the sky! Wow, you really appreciate this beauty!" he said.

"Absolutely! I am praising God for His awesome creation! Do you know Our Creator?" I asked.

"I am Jewish," he said. "That is wonderful" I exclaimed. "Through the Jews, God brought His covenant love to all people, and I am grateful to God and to all Jewish people."

We continued in an amazing conversation and I explained about Jesus, "Yeshua," being a Jew. Michael told me his name meant "like God," and I told him that Yeshua knew him by name and had a purpose for his life.

As he listened curiously, I asked him, "How would you like to hear a story?" He readily agreed, so I told the simple Bible story of Yeshua's encounter with the tax gatherer named Zacchaeus. Michael's curiosity continued as we discussed the story and his faith journey. Considering himself an agnostic, he asked how I could be so sure of my faith.

"When Yeshua changes your life and the lives of many others, there is tangible evidence," I responded. "Plus all the fulfilled prophecies in His Word witness to the Truth," I added.

Evidently, the Spirit of God was drawing him as I gave several examples of God's faithfulness to His covenant people, the Jews.

Michael told me he had never met anyone like me... and was considering what I shared. Willingly he accepted my offer to pray for him, as well as to give him some scriptures to read on his own.

After praying for him to discover for himself who Yeshua was, he hugged me and thanked me for being "a little like God" to him. It's certainly an adventure to be on the journey with God!

Personal Reflection

Read John 1:1-34. Observe how Jesus (Yeshua) is identified and John's role as a witness to the true light. Why do you think the Jewish people did not recognize Jesus (Yeshua) as God's Messiah?

Reflect on John 1:35-51. John called Jesus *the Lamb of God*, Andrew told Simon Peter *We have found the Messiah,* and he brought him to Jesus. Jesus looked at Simon Peter and gave him a new name! He the called Philip and Nathanael to follow Him. They too made declarations about Jesus' identity...*the One Moses and the prophets wrote about in the Law, the Son of God; the King of Israel!*

Respond Jesus told them they would see greater things. *"Very truly I tell you, you will see 'heaven open, and the angels of God ascending and descending on the Son of Man."*

Ask Jesus to reveal greater things about Himself to you. Not only does He know you by name, but He wants you to know Him by Name. His true identity is revealed this way!

Psalm 122:6 commands us to *Pray for the peace of Jerusalem.* The Lord also promises to bless those who bless the nation of Israel and the Jewish people.

"I will bless those who bless you, and whoever curses you I will curse; and all peoples on earth will be blessed through you."
(Genesis 12:3)

73

My Treasured Possession

How intimate is Your call;
Given to one and all;

You have chosen Jacob as your own,
Your faithful love is shown;

How lovely are Your ways,
Guiding us all our days;

Your presence is my joy and delight,
Yeshua, my true light!

My love, my Prince, my King,
Making my heart sing!!

For You,   Lord, have chosen Zion,
To reveal Judah's lion;

Holy Lamb of God so pure,
Promises foretold are sure!

Coming again in glory,
To complete our love story!

Zion is Your resting place,
We will see Your glorious face!

Your glory to be shown
As you sit enthroned!

Blessing forever more,
From Your treasure store!

Higher Ground

Trekking to the top of a mountain in the Arizona desert is exhilarating! Each step leads to my heart pounding faster with eager expectation. Oh, the challenge and the beauty to behold at the top.

Focused and forging ahead, I saw a darling young girl with an adorable dog hiking down the mountain.

"How was the view?" I asked.

"Beautiful," she said, as we continued getting to know each other. Turns out she was trying to sort out her life and direction. She shared her desire for college, but had no clue what to do.

I quickly responded, "No worries, there's someone who does know." With that I shared how my journey to figure out my future led me to a relationship with God. Her interest prompted me to continue my story.

"You see, God is pursuing a relationship with us. In fact, He Knows You by Name and has created you for a purpose. It really is an awesome love story."

Curious, she wanted to hear more. I shared the story of a woman at a well (John 4). After asking the woman for a drink, Jesus shows her how her true thirst can only be quenched by living water that only He, the promised Messiah, can provide, I paralleled it to my searching for purpose and meaning in my image, identity and influence, only to end up empty, with an eating disorder. Somehow I was trying to find my own way to God. Then I was introduced to Jesus Christ as the One who came to bring us to our Creator and Father, God.

"His great love for us led Him to give His life to pay for our sins," I explained. "He paid the debt of our sin so we could live with Him forever! This amazing grace is a gift for all those who will receive Him as their Savior."

Swazey was ready to pray with me to open her heart to Jesus' gift of love and forgiveness. We hugged and exchanged contact information as I encouraged her to learn more of God's love story by reading the Gospel of John. Not only did I make it to higher ground that afternoon, I met a friend to take with me.

Personal Reflection

Read John 4, the story of Jesus' encounter with the woman at a well in Samaria.

Reflect on how Jesus engages with her; using the thirst for water to show how only He can guench our true thirst.

How does Jesus show love and acceptance to her?

In what ways can you relate to her search for satisfaction?

Respond by thanking Him for His unconditional love for each of us! If you have never opened your heart to receive the gift of salvation, you can pray as Swazey and I both did to receive His gift of salvation by simply asking...

"Lord Jesus, I want to know You. Thank You for dying on the cross for my sins. I open the door of my life and receive You as my Savior and Lord. Thank You for forgiving my sins and giving me eternal life. Take control of the throne of my life. Make me the kind of person You want me to be."

with God all things *are possible!*

On Mountain Trail

My eyes behold Your creation,
On this mountain elevation;

Steep the path to bring me here,
Yet you, my love, were very near;

Praying on my way,
"Use me Lord, this day"

Atop the rocks there where I traverse,
Met Swazey to converse.

Seeking the shepherd of her heart,
She prayed to begin a new start.

Opening up to your love,
Surely you are smiling above.

What a glorious victory,
Beginning her forever story.

Grateful to You,
my loving Savior.

Divine Connection Intervention

W ho can imagine what a trip to the local grocery store can produce? The dairy aisle is filled with options. One day, as I scanned the yogurt section, I was presented with the option of responding to the still small voice of the Holy Spirit.

"Nancy, reach out to her." Obediently, I said hello to the woman with her cute little daughter in the cart next to mine. What seemed simple ended up in a story beyond words.

Eager to talk, Jessica was ready to hear a quick story. I told her about living water and the woman who encountered Jesus at the well. He promised her if she drank the water that He gave her, she would never be thirsty again. (John 4).

Jessica liked the story and said she related to that woman. We shared back and forth about our deepest need to be known and loved unconditionally. This resonated with her and before leaving the aisle I shared Jesus' love and care for her and prayed with her that she would discover His love for herself. We exchanged phone numbers and left the store.

I prayed for her and called, but didn't hear back. One evening at a movie, *Cinderella*, I found myself caught up in the beautiful story when a woman with angry voice yelled to the lady with her daughter in front of me.

"Be quiet. We want to watch this movie without your noisy child." Wow, I hadn't really noticed, but this woman was upset. A not-so-nice exchange of words followed, and then another woman from the back silenced them both by shouting, "Shut up."

Well, the drama had only just begun. After the movie, angry women were cursing at each other and pushing each other. It seemed as if a fight would surely start unless someone intervened.

You guessed it. My friend and I entered in to block the fight. I grabbed the woman in front of me and hugged her tightly and whispered in her ear, "It will be okay".

Then she looked at me and said, "Oh my gosh. It is you. You

are the woman I met at the grocery store."

Yes, it was Jessica and her daughter. We couldn't believe it! She was amazed and exclaimed, "You are my Angel!"

Quickly, I led her outside away from the woman who had pushed her and was cursing. As we left she kept saying how she could only imagine what would have happened if I had not been there. A policeman intervened and was willing to trust my counsel not to pursue it further with the other woman.

As we talked and hugged in the parking lot, she agreed it was a divine intervention and agreed to meet me at church in the morning. It was Palm Sunday. After the service I was able to clearly explain the glorious Gospel to her and she invited Jesus to be her Savior and Lord, taking a huge drink of living water that quenched her parched soul. Only the Holy Spirit could have arranged this divine connection and intervention - a TRUE *Cinderella Story* with a Prince forever!

Personal Reflection

Read Luke 15 and notice Jesus' heart to seek and save the lost!

For the Son of Man came to seek and to save the lost.
(Luke 19:10)

Reflect on how God orders our steps and each relationship has a purpose.

In their hearts humans plan their course,
but the Lord establishes their steps.
(Proverbs 16:9)

Respond by praying for each person you meet and obey the prompting of the Holy Spirit. It is surely to be a divine encounter!

Blazing Light

Pierces through the dark night,
with your eternal light;

Bold, bright, electrifying,
all other power defying;

Speak as the Word so true,
You alone can break through;

Any barrier or fear,
causing me to see clear!

You light my way,
and will always stay;

My treasure and my King,
to You my awe I bring;

Forever I will declare
as Your salvation I share!

God can calm the storms in your life.

Garden of Grace

Plans for lunch were cancelled and I had time to spare before my next appointment. "Lord, what shall we do?" I inquired. I felt a desire to go to my favorite prayer garden at San Pedro retreat center.

It was so peaceful and beautiful as I sat soaking in the Lord's presence. Just then, a beautiful young woman walked through the gate and smiled. The Holy Spirit spoke to my heart.

"I have brought you here for her."

"Really, Lord? I wanted to spend time with You!" She walked by and I prayed.

"Whatever you have in mind, Lord, I need Your grace." A few minutes later she came back with a friend. They stopped in front of me, smiling. I marveled at the Lord's clear direction. Engaging with them was so sweet. I discovered Shaloo had a Hindu background and Paloma was from Puerto Rico. Both were at the retreat center for yoga training.

"How would you girls like to hear a beautiful story?" I asked. They nodded curiously.

Again, I told them the story from John 4 about how Jesus met the woman at a well. Through their encounter Jesus addressed the woman's deeper need to drink from the Living Water instead of "temporary waters" that failed to bring her lasting satisfaction. The girls listened to the story intently.

When I asked them what they liked about the story their hearts began to open. They saw how Jesus cared for the woman and how He reached out to her.

"We've never heard this before," they told me. So I briefly shared my own story of how I had searched and tried to satisfy my thirst for purpose in my life. I had their full attention. Knowing the Hindu belief in many gods I shared how Jesus was the promised Savior, God Himself, and how He alone satisfied the longings of my heart.

Our time was so clearly led by the Lord. They both wanted me to pray with them as they opened their hearts to receive Jesus as their Savior and discover more about Him.

This awesome discovery is just beginning for them and I discovered again, that our steps are ordered by the Lord. He knows Shaloo and Paloma by name, and they will never be the same!

He gives us His grace when we listen to the voice of our Good Shepherd who has come to seek and save the lost.

Personal Reflection

Read the story of the Woman at the Well (John 4:1-42).

Reflect on her thirst and what Jesus offered her, living water. Notice how Jesus engages her to help her see her need.

Respond by thanking Him for reaching out to all of us who need to know His unconditional love.

This righteousness is given through faith in Jesus Christ to all who believe. There is no difference between Jew and Gentile, for all have sinned and fall short of the glory of God, and all are justified freely by his grace through the redemption that came by Christ Jesus.
(Romans 3:22-24)

Ask Him who you may tell today, just like the woman who ran back to the town to tell everyone she had ever met. Many came to hear Him and believed!

Longing for You

There's a deep heart cry,
   Without You I die.

Every beat of my heart,
   From the very start;

Was made for you,
   How wonderfully true!

My purpose was planned,
   To grow and expand...

With your divine hand,
   Helping me to stand;

Your presence in me,
   Leading me to see...

"I will give You rest,
   My Glorious best!"

"My beloved, you need not strive,
   Or go into overdrive..."

"Sitting at my feet,
   Intimacy so sweet"

Yes, my Lord, I'll abide,
   Ever at Your right side!

I'll listen for Your voice,
   When making a choice;

My inheritance is in YOU,
   Your covenant reNEW!

The Face of Grace

What a perfect day to refresh my lagging spirit with a swim in the sunshine! It had been a season of some uncertainty and self-doubt. I needed a huge dose of truth from God's Word. Trying to go unnoticed, I covered my eyes with a sun visor and soaked my soul in truths that revived my heart.

After a delightful swim, I was greeted by my neighbor Kathy, who wanted to introduce me to her new friend Lana. Lana was eager to chat and I soon discovered she was visiting her son Paul and his partner Edra.

Meeting Lana was not a coincidence. She opened up to me about the rejection she had experienced from a certain church after her divorce and because of her son's lifestyle. Hungry for hope, she listened as I told the story of Jesus' encounter with Zacchaeus, an unpopular tax collector whom Jesus called out to by name. (Luke 19:1-10). Lana loved the story. She saw how Jesus reached out to Zacchaeus even though others rejected and labeled him.

Lana continued with her story. As I listened, I had an open door to share my story of God's grace as I experienced His acceptance and love in the face of my sin and shame. Just as Zacchaeus was stuck in his lifestyle, I was also in bondage to what others thought and had developed a secret addiction. Only Jesus knew; and when I was in church one day, at my lowest point with a hangover, I heard Him call me by name,

"Nancy do you know me?" I had made it about religion and my performance, but instead He was calling me to a relationship with Himself! What a joy to share with her how I came to know Jesus in a personal way, and how she could too!

The face of grace is shown through each one of our lives as we embrace what Jesus did for us, and share Him with those still searching. Each of our stories is powerful as it shows Jesus' personal love and pursuit of our heart.

*For it is by grace you have been saved, through faith—
and this is not from yourselves, it is the gift of God—
not by works, so that no one can boast.
For we are God's handiwork,
created in Christ Jesus to do good works,
which God prepared in advance for us to do.*
(Ephesians 2:8-10)

Personal Reflection

Read the story of Zacchaeus (Luke 19:1-10).

Reflect on Jesus' invitation to Zacchaeus, despite his reputation and sin.

Respond by praying for people you many know who are caught in a simple lifestyle. He may use you to reach out and invite them into a personal relationship with Him.

Shepherd of My Soul

*You promised to lead me,
Where my heart is free;*

*You know me by name,
No two sheep the same;*

*May I listen for your voice.
And follow by my choice;*

*For your pastures are green,
And ways no eye has seen;*

*No ear has heard it all,
Except by your Spirit call;*

*What our Father has prepared,
For those His life was shared;*

*Yeshua, Shepherd of my soul,
In You alone I am whole!*

Sweet Spot

S weet Mama's is a charming country café that is perfect for a cup of coffee and a discussion about anything.

In the course of a meeting while sitting at the counter, our sweet waitress went off duty. When a big guy with tattoos poured a refill of my coffee, I spontaneously asked,

"Oh, are you Sweet Papa?" We laughed and began a fun conversation.

I asked Julio if he wanted to hear a story.

"Why not?" he said as he put the coffee pot down. It was fun to tell him the story of Bartimaeus, a blind beggar who called to Jesus from the side of the road. Jesus took notice and told him to come. Friends helped him go to Jesus. He was never the same after Jesus asked him, "Bartimaeus, what do you want me to do for you?"

"Teacher, I want to see!" Miraculously, his sight was restored and he followed Jesus.

Julio loved the story. He had never heard it before. I asked him, "If Jesus asked you, what you wanted Him to do for you what would you say?" He began to open up to me about his life and his problems with drugs and alcohol. He said he wanted Jesus to help him. Wow! How could I have known his desperate need? But, Jesus did! There are no accidents with Him. I was in the right place at right time, by God's design.

Julio heard how Jesus could forgive him and set him free, as I intertwined my own testimony along with Bartimaeus' story. I shared the Gospel of Grace and salvation with him and Sweet Mama's became a place of sweet surrender as Julio prayed with me to receive Jesus into his heart that afternoon. What a "divine coincidence" followed when a big burly brother in Christ came in at that very moment. Pastor Barry was just the right man to help Julio take the next step in his faith journey.

Jesus knew where the "Sweet Spot" was, because He is the sweetest name I know! I am savoring these sweet surprises of His supernatural leading.

Personal Reflection

Read the story of the Bartimaeus found in Mark 10:46-52.

Reflect on your own life. What would you like to ask Jesus to do for you? Don't be afraid to ask Him. He Knows You by Name and cares for you.

Respond by reaching out today to others who may need to hear this story, and ask them what they would like Jesus to do for them. Just maybe you will sweeten their lives by introducing them to Jesus!

Let Your Glory Shine

Awesome King of all,
Let them hear your call;

May your light shine,
In all hearts and mine;

Show us the way,
On this blessed day;

We are here by design,
Let us be Your sign;

The King calls you by name,
No more fear or shame;

Open hearts to receive,
And humbly believe;

Jesus is the only way,
Reveal to them I pray!

Freely Receive, Freely Give

L ooking forward to my favorite place to stop for gas, I pulled in eager to try the free yogurt samples. Getting my white chocolate mocha coffee, I noticed one of the sales girls. A fleeting prayer came into my heart.

"Lord, can you use me in her life to tell her about Your love," but then she disappeared in the back.

Greeted by two nice guys at the cash register, I was surprised when they smiled and said, "This one's on us."

"Wow, that's a blessing! I only know one other free gift... that is the love of Jesus. Do you know Him?"

"Yes," they both responded but seemed curious. As I shared how I came to know Jesus in personal way versus simply trying to be religious, they listened attentively and received my story with enthusiasm.

Just then, the girl I had briefly met at the counter returned. She had obviously heard part of the conversation, so I asked her name.

"Carina," she responded.

"What about you, do you know anything about Jesus' love?"

"No, I don't."

"Would you like to hear a really cool story about another woman who met Jesus?"

"Yes, I would."

It was clear to me the Lord was pursuing her. Once again, I used the story of Jesus' encounter with the woman at the well in John 4, to capture her attention. She liked the story; and as we discussed it she realized that Jesus was caring for a woman just like her! Telling her that I had felt I was supposed to talk with her seemed to touch her heart. I shared my story about how I met Jesus at age 19 (around her age), and she willingly agreed to read a little booklet I wrote called "My Story," which includes the Gospel. She agreed to give me her opinion the next time I stopped in to fill my car with gas and receive a lot more than free coffee...for Jesus does know each one of us by name.

Personal Reflection

Read the story of Jesus encounter with a woman from Samaria, in John 4:1-42.

Reflect on noticing how Jesus engaged this woman at the well, even though there were racial tensions between the Jews and Samaritans.

How did He reach out to her? Did He show respect and interest in her? Was He intentional in relating to her?

What really touched her heart? Did Jesus show any condemnation of her, or did He seem to value her despite her background?

Did He clearly communicate who He was?

Respond by asking Jesus to give you a heart to reach out to engage people in conversations that shows you care and are truly interested in them.

Observe how your love for them can open their hearts to hear about the One who loves them more than any human ever could, and can provide them with the living water that wells up to eternal life.

Pray that He will give you eyes to see the opportunities before you every day, and enjoy the adventure of being His ambassador!

My Beloved

May our hearts receive,
And come to believe...

Your love and affection,
Guiding our direction;

"My peace I give to You"
Your promise that is true!

Thank you, Our God and Father,
You are like no other!

You created and called each one,
Uniquely designed to know your Son!

Long ago Your plan was laid,
Now the purchase price is paid;

Our Prince of Peace made the way,
May we each discover Your love, I pray!

To every heart that is broken,
May Your comfort be spoken;

"Come to me,"
And You will see...

He knows Your Name,
You will never be the same!

Fresh Encounter

What divine timing for the seeking Savior to send me to encounter Mike who was relaxing in the swimming lane next to me.

Mike was a big lively guy, a chef, and so hungry for the truth. A friendly greeting with a question about where he was from opened his heart. After discovering his Thai background, I offered him a Jesus film in his language, which turned out to be English! Smile...only Thai roots, he'd never been there. He was fascinated that I had.

He asked about it and gave me the opportunity to tell my story of meeting Jesus through investigating religion. "Buddha is dead...Jesus is alive!" I summarized with a smile.

He kept saying "Amazing," so I told him the story of Bartimaeus' encounter with Jesus.

"Wow! Amazing!" he said again. He knew nothing and wanted to know more. Only God, our Father could prepare him so perfectly to meet His Son. After hearing Bartimaeus' story he wanted to know how I met Jesus. Step by step I shared my journey of discovering God's amazing grace. I told him there are four truths in the Bible that really helped me to understand.

"Can you tell me?" he asked.

After sharing the beautiful grace-full gospel, he was so eager to pray with me to receive Jesus for Himself! Angels rejoiced with us! We shook hands and I blessed him with a prayer. He thanked me for this "amazing discovery."

Gladly he received the book of John and "My Story," my little booklet with my testimony and the gospel, along with the Jesus film and an invitation to church, all of which he accepted eagerly. What a joy to join Jesus - as He seeks and saves the lost as a shepherd looking for that one lost sheep until he's found! Mike, the Thai chef, is now a son of the Most High God. His journey has just begun.

Personal Reflection

Read John Chapter 3 and notice the conversation between Jesus and Nicodemus.

Reflect Consider your own story. How did Jesus encounter you? Did someone share His love and grace with you? Were you seeking Him or did He seek you?

Respond by thanking God for your journey wherever you are on this path to know Jesus. Invite Him to reveal more of His heart to you.

> *"No one can come to me unless*
> *the Father who sent me draws them,*
> *and I will raise them up at the last day."*
> (John 6:44)

Consider how God can use you, who have freely received, to freely share of His love, good news and grace. Then pray and ask Him to lead you.

Fresh Encounter

Some days my heart is faint,
Not feeling at all like a saint!

Hungry for your touch of grace,
I set out to seek your face;

What happens is amazing to me,
For in Your holy presence I see;

Empty though my cup may be,
You show up beautifully;

Leading me to others to hear,
I sense your love so dear!

In telling your love story,
I see your matchless glory!

Now it is for you to reveal,
Restore, deliver and heal.

Pursuing love, gather them to You,
Making their hearts brand new!

Once again, I am renewed,
Because your love has pursued.

I See Your Deepest Hunger

Who wouldn't enjoy baklava and other tasty Middle Eastern treats? How special when our host, in Nazareth, invited my friends and I to his favorite bakery. We were greeted with such warmth and hospitality and the owner immediately brought delicious mouth-watering desserts to our table. Our charming waiter was delighted with our response of gratitude and joy!

"Wow! This reminds me of one of my favorite stories where food showed up unexpectedly," I exclaimed. After our waiter had finished serving us, I asked, "Would you like to hear it?"

Just then the owner came out and suggested, "How about coming back to the kitchen to share your story with all the bakers and you can see the cooking process too." All of our group agreed that it sounded like fun.

The owner was pleased we were enjoying our scrumptious desserts and wanted to show us more gracious hospitality. What an experience seeing these chefs in action! They were all smiles as they took us step by step from kneading the dough, twisting it, to filling it with yummy nuts and dates and then baking it.

The proud owner had not forgotten my offer to tell a story. He gathered all the cooks together (about fifteen) to listen as our guide translated for me.

"As soon as Jesus heard the news that his cousin John the Baptist had been beheaded, he left in a boat to a remote area to be alone. But the crowds heard where he was headed and followed on foot from many towns. Jesus saw the huge crowd as he stepped from the boat. He had compassion on them and healed the sick. That evening the disciples came to him and said, "This is a remote place, and it's already getting late. Send the crowds away so they can go to the villages and buy food for themselves."

But Jesus said, "That isn't necessary...you feed them."

"But we have only five loaves of bread and two fish," they answered.

"Bring them here," He said. Then He told the people to sit down on the grass. Jesus took the five loaves and two fish, looked up toward heaven and blessed them. Then, breaking the loaves into pieces, He gave the bread to the disciples who distributed it to the people. They all ate as much as they wanted and afterward, the disciples picked up twelve baskets of leftovers. About 5,000 men were fed that day, in addition to all the women and children."

Our new friends, the cooks, the waiter and the owner loved the story and said they hadn't heard it before. Since they were so engaged, I continued sharing with them about how Jesus not only met the physical needs of people, but also called himself "the Bread of Life." He knew the deepest hunger of our hearts and promised that if we ate the bread He gave, we would never be hungry again. It was clearly touching their hungry hearts as they listened closely! I shared a little of my own quest for satisfaction and how I met Jesus personally. It was a divine moment to share with them the Bread of Life, Jesus.

I ended by offering a brief prayer asking Jesus to reveal Himself to them and inviting them to open their hearts to receive His love and forgiveness.

They all clapped and thanked us very much. We gave each of them a Jesus film in their language to learn more. It was truly a picture of His bread being multiplied to hungry hearts.

Personal Reflection

Read several accounts of this miracle story in John 6:1-14, Luke 9:10–17 and Mark 6:30-44.

Reflect on the miracle and how Jesus cared about their physical and spiritual needs.

Respond by asking Him to use you to be His hands and feet as you show His love and compassion to those in need!

Pray for open doors to introduce others to Jesus, who can satisfy the deepest hunger in their hearts.

Valley of Decision

My sacrificial Savior and Lord,
So many have not yet heard;

Your blood has paid the price,
For them to be born twice.

Salvation is Your Name,
To You all honor and fame.

Nations will come to Your Glory,
A vctorious love story.

Enlarge the place of my tent,
On this, my heart is bent.

Cords to be lengthened,
Stakes will be strengthened;

Spreading Your love far and wide,
As I humbly abide;

Nations will come to Your Light,
Your promises become sight.

Descendants shall inherit, Your fire,
As they boldly aspire.

My husband is my maker and King.
His Name is Lord of Everything.

All glory and honor to Yeshua, My King.
His expectant Bride, Nancy

(Inspired by Isaiah 54)

Abraham, Called by God

"How much are these bracelets," I asked a shop owner in Nazareth. "Oh, and what is your name?"

"Abraham" he answered.

"Wow, the Father of Faith!"

He smiled knowingly. He was of Muslim descent.

"Do you know much about why he was called "Father of Faith?" I told him the story of Abraham and Sarah having a baby and then God asking Abraham to offer his only son to God. Amazingly, he was not busy at that moment and his obvious interest led me to go on with the story. "Abraham obeyed and trusted God as he prepared to offer his son as a sacrifice. God miraculously intervened and stopped him, providing a ram in place of his son."

What an opportunity I had to explain how God our Father had offered His only son Jesus as a sacrifice for our sins. Abraham was listening attentively as I continued by explaining how Jesus had not only died, but had risen from the dead, showing His victory over sin and death so that we could have eternal life.

My time with Abraham was a divine moment of conversation before people came into his shop. Before I left, I was able to pray a short prayer over him as he agreed to explore more about Jesus! God was calling Abraham by name! He was single, so I told him I would also pray for his "Sarah" and for him to become a father of many called by God.

He gave me a small gift from his shop, a beautiful stone.

Personal Reflection

Read Genesis 22. Observe God's clear instructions and Abraham's immediate obedience.

Reflect upon Abraham's confidence that *God Himself would provide the lamb for the burnt offering* (Genesis 22:8)

Respond by praying that people of many faith backgrounds would see clearly that *Jesus is the Lamb of God, who takes away the sins of the world!* (John 1:29)

97

Sacrificial Lamb of God

You rescued me and mankind,
One desperate sinner to find;

Your sacrifice opened the way,
For a bright new glorious day!

I'm continually in awe of You,
My Redeemer and friend so true;

You rescued me for eternity,
One day my eyes will fully see;

May I never stop seeking,
And humbly believing...

Every heart that beats,
Your grace completes!

As I take your truth to all,
May I share your loving call;

Every heart needs your cure,
Only you make them secure;

You have designed me for your glory,
To boldly tell your love story!

Gratefully going with You,
Your Ambassador

Chosen by God

"**D**o not be afraid, Mary, you have found favor with God," the angel told her, "You will conceive and give birth to a son, and you are to call him Jesus." (Luke 1:30-31)

I can only imagine the wonder Mary experienced as God's angel messenger greeted her so personally and specifically. As with Mary, He knows each one of us by name and has a plan and purposes for our life. Our response means everything in determining whether or not we will fulfill our calling.

Mary responded, *"I am the Lord's servant. May it be to me as you have said."* (Luke 1:38) May we, too, respond as Mary did.

As I sat outside the place where the angel appeared to Mary, an excited group of Chinese pilgrims came to the courtyard. Their tour guide was frantically trying to find out where they were to go for Catholic Mass. The Lord prompted me to step in and offer to share this story to these precious tourists. A sweet Chinese lady translated. They eagerly listened as I shared not only about the angel coming to Mary, but how the Lord had encountered me personally at the age of 19 to follow Him fully as My Lord and Savior.

During that divine moment He once again called me by name. This time to let Him use me as His messenger. What an honor to listen for His call.

Personal Reflection

Read Luke 1:26-38 (the account of the angel coming to Mary).

Reflect on Mary's response to the angel, *"I am the Lord's servant."* Mary answered, *"May your word to me be fulfilled."* Then the angel left her.

How do you think she felt? In awe? afraid? confused? Why do you think God chose Mary?

Respond by thanking God for coming to this earth to take on our humanity, and understand all of our human challenges and struggles!

Ask Him to show you more about how He has chosen you to know Him and fulfill the purpose He has created you for.

For he chose us in him before the creation of the world to be holy and blameless in his sight. In love he predestined us for adoption to sonship through Jesus Christ, in accordance with his pleasure and will— to the praise of his glorious grace, which he has freely given us in the One he loves.
(Ephesians 1:4-6)

Allow God to create in you a humble, trusting heart as He reveals His perfect will for your life. The more you get to know Him, the easier it is to trust Him with your life!

Accept His gift of grace to you. Invite Jesus into your heart as your Savior if you have not done so already.

For it is by grace you have been saved, through faith—and this is not from yourselves, it is the gift of God—not by works, so that no one can boast. For we are God's handiwork, created in Christ Jesus to do good works, which God prepared in advance for us to do.
(Ephesians 2:8-10)

Night in Nazareth

Lights shining in the night,
Remind me of the true light;

Here is where the angel came,
Nothing would ever be the same!

Mary humbly received her call,
And gave the Lord her all;

Light of the world stepped down,
And glory shown all around;

He grew to be a young man,
Favor with man, at God's right hand;

Yeshua loved and served all,
Knowing His divine call;

Divinity wrapped in humility
A carpenter of nobility.

Then His time did come,
He spoke with such wisdom.

Wasn't He Mary and Joseph's son?
But this season of life was done.

Yeshua began to preach,
He had the lost to reach.

My heart rejoices tonight,
He came and gave me sight.

My beloved Savior and King,
To You all worship and thanks I bring.

Tonight in Nazareth, I rejoice,
In Your Holy awesome choice;

To give your life for mine,
Forever your light will shine.

Named with a Purpose

We are from the town of Cana, the two college age guys told my friends and me. "Do you know the miracle that happened there," they asked.

"Yes, I've heard about it, but would love to hear you tell us!" I responded.

With excitement, they recounted Jesus' experience at the wedding in Cana when the wine ran out and Jesus' mother Mary told the servants to do whatever Jesus told them. He honored His mother's request and to the amazement of all there, the water in the jars turned to the best wine ever.

Our two new friends were so impressed with Jesus' miracle that I asked if they knew any other miracles of Jesus.

"No," they said and added, "Do you?"

"Absolutely! Do you want to hear one?" I offered.

"Yes! Tell us!" they answered enthusiastically.

Before I began the story I asked their names. One was named Magdy, meaning "glory" and the other was named Tarik meaning "shining bright light."

"Wow! What special names God has given you. I think He wants you both to shine with His glory!" I suggested with joy.

They smiled as I began the story of Jesus healing a paralytic who had been lowered through the rooftop by his four friends. When Jesus saw their faith, He told the paralyzed friend "Take courage, your sins are forgiven."

"As the story continues," I told them, "Jesus not only forgives his sins, but heals him totally. He walks out in front of everyone and all are amazed and praising God.

"What do you think of this story?" I asked Magdy and Tarik.

"He forgave him his sins."

This led to a wonderful discussion about Jesus ability and authority to forgive sins. Being from a Muslim background, this was a radical truth to consider, so we encouraged Magdy and Tarik to ask God to reveal to them who Jesus is - just a prophet or more?

We prayed with them and left our new friends knowing Jesus knew them by name and had chosen them to know Him by name and to shine His glory on others.

Personal Reflection

Read the story of the paralyzed man (Mark 2:1-12).

Reflect on the miracle and the message, *your sins are forgiven* that show Jesus' authority and power. Notice how Jesus' divine miracles all reveal His deity.

Respond by asking Jesus to let His glory shine in and through you as you learn to tell His story along with your story!

Let Your Glory Shine

Awesome King of all,
Let them hear your call;

May your light shine,
In all hearts and mine;

Show us the way,
On this blessed day;

We are here my design,
Let us be your sign;

The King calls you by name,
No more fear or shame;

Open hearts to receive,
And humbly believe;

Jesus is the only way,
Reveal to them I pray!

Lost and Found

I've always been directionally challenged so I made sure to have clear notes of my bus transfers from Galilee to Nazareth! What fun to meet new Israeli friends on the bus, all the while checking with the bus driver about my stop.

After three checks I figured he would remember, but when I asked he said,

"Oh no, I passed it up! I am so sorry! You can get off here and cross over and catch the next bus back to where you were supposed to be." Sounded so easy to him, but my not knowing Hebrew made me very unsure.

Then he decided to take me back himself, but people began to yell at him in Hebrew. They had places to go and people to see, too! I quickly said,

"Don't worry. The Lord will take care of me and I got off the bus with a scribbled note from the driver. "Oh Lord, I need some angelic assistance." I prayed as I got to the next bus stop a darling young Israeli guy helped me get on the right bus! Only a Chinese girl and I were on it besides Adam, our young Arab driver. It seemed set up by God because my new Chinese friend had come to Israel to seek God, and Adam was speaking fluent English and agreed to take us both where we needed to go.

"Adam," I asked, "Have you met your Eve yet?"

"Not yet," he smiled.

"Well, you are very kind to help Shi-Shi and me by 'going the extra mile!" How would you like to hear a true story about something amazing that happened in this area?" I asked. He was up for it, along with Shi-Shi.

I began, "One day Jesus was teaching and some friends wanted to bring their paralyzed friend to Him. It was crowded. They could not get in, so they tore a hole in the roof and lowered him right in front of Jesus." I continued with this amazing story of Jesus forgiving the paralytic's sins and healing him completely in front of many religious leaders and people.

As Adam and I talked about the story, he said he really liked that Jesus forgave the man's sins! We discussed many things about Jesus that day. My being lost ended up with Jesus leading me to two other lost people who were so open to hear the truth. When we arrived at our stop I was able to encourage Adam to read more in the B'Rit Hadashah (New Testament) to discover who Jesus is. Shi-Shi and I ended up spending the day together. She also was a seeker being found by Jesus. Who would have thought that Jesus would use a lost girl, like me, to find two precious people He knows by name to help them find Him. Only our Good Shepherd!

Personal Reflection

Read John 14:1-14 Focus on...

> *"I am the way and the truth and the life.*
> *No one comes to the Father except through me."*
> (John 14:6)

Reflect on Jesus' heart mission. In John 14:12 He tells us that anyone who has faith in Him will do what He has been doing and even greater things...because He is going to the Father.

Respond by asking Him to show you who He is, if you are lost and don't know the way. If you know Jesus, ask Him to use you to lead others to Him.

> *"For the Son of Man came to seek and to save the lost."*
> (Luke 19:10)

Time Is Short

No time to hesitate,
The hour is so late.

Jesus, our Savior came,
Not in glorious fame...

His purpose to die
For you and I.

Salvation full and free,
May the world see.

For He is coming to reign,
Our King has made it plain.

We must prepare the way,
For this soon coming day.

Many have been deceived,
And have not believed.

Our mission is clear,
For soon He will appear.

Clothed in glorious light;
To pierce the dark night.

Don't hesitate to proclaim,
His beautiful NAME.

For harvest time is now,
One day all will bow.

Jesus is Lord of ALL,
At His feet we will fall.

Beautiful Name

W hat a delightful day in Jerusalem to have lunch out- side, enjoying my friends. Glancing at all the people, I noticed that a woman seated alone at the table next to us. I smiled and said, "Shalom." We began to talk and soon I was seated at her table getting to know her. Her name was Yaffa meaning "beau- tiful."

Little did I know that she was struggling with her health that day. When I asked about her life she told me she had no chil- dren, but had two miscarriages. Though she assured me she was fine, I could detect there was more to the story. She asked about me and I told her I loved to share true stories of how God cares about each of us. Venturing out I asked if I could tell her one.

"Yes, of course," she said.

"One day Yeshua was traveling through town with a large crowd following Him because of all the miracles He was doing, including healing many people. There was a woman in the crowd who had been bleeding for twelve years. No doctor could help her and she had spent all her money trying to get well."

She listened closely as I told her how the woman thought,

"If only I can touch His cloak, I will be healed." I continued the story, "She then pushed through the crowd and reached out to touch the edge of His robe. Immediately her bleeding stopped.

Yeshua asked, "Who touched me?"

"How can we know?" the friends asked. "Everyone is pressing in around You."

"I know," Yeshua said. "Power has gone out from Me."

The woman realizing she could not go unnoticed, came trem- bling before Him telling Him what happened.

Yeshua said to her, "Daughter, your faith has healed you. Go in peace."

Yaffa said, "I like this man!"

"Do you know anything about Him?" I asked.

She didn't, saying she was more secular and believed all religions led to God.

We discussed God's love and care for us and how He knows each one of us intimately. I explained that He sent His Son Yeshua to this earth to take our pain, suffering and sin upon Himself by dying in our place.

All this was new to her, but she began to open her heart more to me by revealing her use of marijuana to help her deal with her pain. I took her hand and told her He understood and cared about her.

I also shared my story of meeting Yeshua and how He healed me of emotional pain and delivered me from addiction. She said she liked me, and it was good to talk and share. By the time we said good bye, I prayed for her to experience Yeshua's love for her and to discover who He is. We had laughed and opened our hearts to each other. Yaffa smiled and thanked me. Truly, Yeshua knew her by name. Yaffa is beautiful to Him and He sent my beautiful feet to reach out to her to reveal His love and care for her.

How beautiful on the mountains are the feet
of those who bring good news.
(Isaiah 52:7)

Personal Reflection

Read Luke 8:40-55 and experience the healing love of Jesus.

Reflect on the woman's anguish and shame at her condition. Imagine her desperation that led her to take such a courageous step. Reach out to believe Him for yourself and others. How many in our culture are needing the hope and healing that Jesus offers?

Respond in praise at how Jesus healed and restored the woman's dignity as He called her "Daughter."

What need do you or someone you know face today that only He can heal? Reach out to Him in bold faith.

Gracious Father

My grace-filled giver of ALL,
To You, I humbly call;

You see me at this hour,
Send Your Holy Spirit's power;

Break through my chains,
To where my Jesus reigns.

Seated royally on His throne,
His glory eternally shone!

My Beloved Savior is my ALL,
At His pierced feet I fall;

He tenderly lifts my chin,
"My daughter, I paid for your sin.

Rejoice, oh daughter, sing for joy,
Your enemy, I did destroy!

Shout triumphantly, daughter of Zion,
I am coming soon as a roaring Lion!

To gather My precious Bride,
Forever to remain at My side.

Keep your eyes on Me,
Holy wonders, you will see."

Crossing the Cultural Divide

W alking the beautiful boardwalk in Haifa one evening, I noticed a young woman busy with her phone. I passed by with a prayer for her.

The next morning I was enjoying a brisk walk on the same promenade. Only this time, the same young woman was there smoking a cigarette while she waited for her salon to open. Spontaneously, I greeted her with a smile, and she was happy to speak English with me.

Gil was Jewish and knew who Yeshua was, but not much about Him.

I asked, "Would you enjoy hearing a story, while you wait?" She answered in the affirmative and agreed to tell me what she thought. As I told her the story of Yeshua's encountering a woman at a well in Samaria where typically Jews didn't engage with Samaritans, she listened intently. When I asked her what she liked about the story she responded quickly.

"I liked that He accepted this woman, though she was from a different background." Gil opened up to me about a relationship she was having with a young Arab man from a Muslim background. She expressed the difficulty she was having because of her parents disappointment, and lit up another cigarette.

"You see, she explained, they are very religious Jews."

As we continued to discuss the story, we talked about the way Yeshua reached out to the woman. He obviously knew all about her. The conversation turned to a personal discussion about how neither she nor her boyfriend were religious, so they didn't understand why it was a problem for them to be together.

Gil listened curiously as I shared my own story of searching many places and then discovering a personal relationship with God through Yeshua. We talked about the living water that would satisfy her heart and soul. I told her that the deepest need of our lives cannot be met by another person, but only by Him, the One who created us and loves us unconditionally.

"Maybe you and your boyfriend can discover more about Him! Yeshua crosses all cultures. He came to the Jew first, but He also came for all people, including the Muslims," I told her.

Gil accepted a DVD with the story of Yeshua in multiple languages. We agreed to meet again later so I could introduce her to my friends in Haifa. I marveled at Yeshua's care for her. Knowing her struggle and reaching out to her made me love Him even more.

Personal Reflection

Read Ephesians 2:11-22. Observe how Jesus came to bridge the cultural divide and create "one new man" through His death on the cross.

Reflect on how you can be an instrument of peace and healing as you share His love with both Jews and Gentiles.

Respond by confessing any prejudice or pride you may have in your heart towards people of different races or religions.

Ask Jesus to fill you with His love and compassion for all people as you reach out with the Good News of the Gospel.

you are what God knows you are!

Thy Kingdom Come

Far away in a distant land,
Without time, earth or sand;

Lives the matchless King of Kings,
For whom my heart sings.

He has told us of His return,
And daily I seek to learn;

How I want to be ready,
Honoring Him firm and steady;

Filled with eager anticipation,
For He alone is my expectation;

My life, my breath, my very being,
Oh, how I love Him without seeing;

Prince Yeshua has captured my heart,
Passionately in love from the start;

He gave His life, His all;
How can I not heed His call?

I am His Beloved Bride,
Ever to reign at His side;

But now... there are nations to hear,
People and loved ones far and near;

I will traverse His glorious earth,
Proclaiming and bringing new birth.

Going together with My King,
Wearing His covenant ring.

Festival of Lights

My cup overflowed. Joy and celebration filled the air as my friend and I joined in the "Festival of Lights" in Jerusalem.

We asked the man serving Italian cappuccino for a cup of coffee, it sounded delicious.

"How about a story," I asked him while waiting.

"Sure, why not," he replied.

Since we were in Jerusalem, it was fun to tell a story set in Jericho about a blind man named Bartimaeus who met Yeshua and was miraculously healed of his blindness!

"That is my name; Joshua (Yeshua) means salvation," he exclaimed! "Cool," I responded.

"Do you know much about him?" I asked.

He said, "I know he did a lot of good things."

As Joshua continued serving coffee, we went on with our conversation about who Yeshua was and is.

Just then three high school girls, Maya, Ruth and Tal came to order a drink. They said they knew a story about Yeshua and how he raised a little girl from the dead! Talitha Kum was the name of a church near them which means *My Child Arise*. Since they didn't know the full story, I told it to them. (Luke 8:40-55). I sensed that Yeshua was touching their hearts as they listened to the story with eagerness and loved it.

Their sweet hearts were so open when they told me about some of the pressures they were experiencing in school and the fact that their faith was important to them. I responded by sharing my own story of coming to know Yeshua in a personal way and how He helped me to experience His peace and acceptance that really freed me. They were quite interested. What an overflowing cup of coffee we shared! The girls received **My Story**, a little booklet with my story and His story to take with them to explain more about Yeshua's love for them. What a joy to see His revealing of Himself to them. My heart was freshly reminded that He Joshua, Maya, Ruth, Tal and knows each one of us by name.

Personal Reflection

Read Luke 8:40-55 and observe how the entire community experienced this miracle.

Reflect on this miracle. What does it show us about the power Yeshua had over life and death?

Think about how these miracle stories are able to captivate people with the reality of who Yeshua is and give them a desire to know more about Him.

Respond by learning to tell this story and others found in the Gospels so you can share them with people who may not know much about Jesus (Yeshua).

Hope

What remains when all seems dark?
Will we ever hear the lark?

Seasons come and go;
Wanting to let us know;

Each seed bears a kernel,
Rooted in the eternal;

Nature pictures all that is
Birthed in wisdom, only His;

Though we now dimly see,
He holds time and eternity;

Our lives though fragile and brief.
Can bring is despair and grief;

Only when we lift our eyes
To the One who hears our cries;

Can we then begin to believe,
And of His hope we can receive.

Shabbat Shalom

"**P**eace to you this Shabbat!" is a common greeting beginning at sundown on Friday and continuing through sundown on Saturday for the Jewish people. "Shabbat Shalom."

I greeted Arnold, an 85-year-old Jewish man I met walking on a Florida beach one Saturday morning. He was happy to stop and visit as I expressed my love for Israel and the Jewish people. Showing him the Scripture I was meditating on as I was walking, we began a lengthy conversation.

I read him parts of Psalm 89 about God's covenant with David. "*I have found David my servant, with my sacred oil I have anointed him.*" (v. 20) God promises: "*I will maintain my love to him forever, and my covenant with him will never fail. I will establish his line forever, his throne as long as the heavens endure.*" (vs. 28-29)

Arnold was touched by my love and interest in Israel and the Jewish people. I explained how I came to understand the privilege I have as a believer in Yeshua (Jesus) to be grafted into the covenant established through Abraham. We talked further about all the Jewish feasts, and I was able to share how I celebrate them too and how they have enriched my faith! It seemed as if the Lord had given Arnold and me a bond and he was genuinely open to hearing more of Yeshua.

As the Holy Spirit led me, I shared about Yeshua's being a Jew who came to His people, but they didn't recognize Him as their Messiah because He came to die as the sacrificial Lamb of God. This is foretold in Isaiah 53.

I added, "He is coming again as the King to rule and reign in Zion. All of this is foretold in Zechariah 8-12 and other places in God's Word.

We also discussed the spiritual challenges in Israel and the battle between Satan and God. I was able to tell him that all the first disciples of Yeshua were Jews and that they all died martyrs deaths after His resurrection.

What an amazing conversation I had with this dear man who at 85 years of age walks four miles each day, though his precious wife, Jane, is in poor health. I assured him I would pray for her to have perfect Shalom, which in Hebrew means wholeness, completeness and wellness. I explained to him that one of Yeshua's names is Sar Shalom, Prince of Peace! When I pray for someone's life or pray Shalom for the peace of Jerusalem, I am calling upon Yeshua to reign and rule.

We ended our beach visit with a blessing. He gave me a hug, and I prayed over him,

> *The Lord bless you and keep you;*
> *The Lord make his face shine upon you*
> *and be gracious to you;*
> *The Lord turn his face toward you and give you peace.*
> (Numbers 6:24-26)

As we said good-bye, I encouraged him to ask Adonai (the Lord God) if Yeshua was the Messiah and to read Isaiah 53. He willingly gave me his phone number and address so that I could mail him a book called "I Have a Friend Who's Jewish. Do You?"

I'm praying Arnold will meet the most precious friend I know, Yeshua, the Messiah and soon coming King.

Personal Reflection

Read and experience the story of the Jewish synagogue leader and the miracle healing of his daughter in Luke 8:40-56.

Reflect on God's name in Hebrew, "Yahweh Shalom," the Lord is Peace and our "Sar Shalom," the Prince of Peace Yeshua.

Respond by praying for opportunities to reach out to Jewish people and people of different religious backgrounds.

Savoring Yeshua

Diving mystery to see,
Yeshua came for you and me;

Wrapped in cloth as an infant,
Abba, Father graciously sent;

Beautiful life of love and grace;
Seeing Yahweh in Yeshua's face;

So kind, powerful and pure,
Evidence His deity so sure.

What a perfect life He lived
Though He came, His life to give;

Bearing the world's sin,
All that has ever been;

On the cross He died,
Heaven and earth cried.

Oh, but death where is your sting?
Let all creation's praises ring.

Three days in the grave,
For all mankind to save.

Miriam found the stone rolled away.
Angels in white where He once lay.

Yeshua called her name,
She would never be the same.

"I have seen the Lord," she proclaimed.
Forever unashamed.

Celebrating victory!

A Message for You

M arco Island, Florida, has a gorgeous beach. After writing all morning I decided to walk the beach and pray. When I saw a young man on his cell phone a thought came to me. "God has a message for him; I wonder if he has ever heard it?" I waited for him to finish his call, but in spite of the thundering waves and wind he continued talking.

A storm was brewing, so I interrupted him to tell him I had a message for him. I offered him a DVD on the life of Jesus.

Shaking his head, he said he wasn't interested. I walked away wondering how many of us miss God's messages because we are too preoccupied with all the other voices in our lives! Has God tried to message you unsuccessfully lately? Or have you been the messenger who has felt less than "well-received?"

Remember, God took great lengths to reach us. He came down from heaven to seek and save us. He knew some would reject Him. He showed His great love. Even though we were His enemies, He died for us.

Don't ever fear someone who will not receive the message you are sent to deliver. You may just be getting a "busy" signal, and someone will be sent to try again later.

Personal Reflection

Read Matthew 18:10-14.

Reflect upon how the Lord has patiently pursued you. Thank Him for His heart to go after the lost sheep.

Respond by praying for someone you know who needs to hear the message of God's unconditional love and forgiveness. Ask if you may be His messenger.

Am I now trying to win the approval of human beings, or of God? Or am I trying to please people? If I were still trying to please people, I would not be a servant of Christ.
(Galatians 1:10)

Master Designer

Each one created and crafted by You,
How I wish they all knew...

Everyday ordained to be,
Even though some don't see;

Beautifully led by Your hand,
Helping me to firmly stand;

Ever strong by Your grace,
Fixing my gaze upon Your face;

I am Yours, You are mine,
With Your light, I will shine;

Intimacy with You to the end,
Running the race that You send;

Teach me to be still and know,
Your Holy Spirit's flow...

As my heart longs for all,
To receive His gracious call!

Partnering with You, my Savior,
Your Beloved Bride

Shiny Shells

My eyes caught the glimmer of little shiny shells as I walked the beach. I couldn't help but stop since they stood out amidst the duller shells. Upon inspection, I noticed they seemed to be light and iridescent. Carefully collecting some, I placed them in my bag!

Walking farther, I saw a family with several children. The Lord prompted me to offer them a wonderful gift, the same DVD I wanted to give to the young man on the phone.

They saw the DVD was the story of Jesus and were happy to receive it. The children were especially glad about it. I told them how much Jesus loved them and how He welcomed them with love and blessings. Smiling, I engaged them and their parents in conversation.

"I have another gift for you," I told them. "I've been collecting 'shiny shells,' would you like one?"

Eagerly they each took one, and then, just as quickly the little girl said, "And I have a present for you." She handed me a shell she had collected!

After enjoying their delightful, spontaneous joy, I went on my way, praising Jesus!

"Lord," I said, "Make me as 'shiny' for you as these children are. For Jesus said, *"Truly I tell you, unless you change and become like little children, you will never enter the kingdom of heaven."* (Matthew 18:3)

Personal Reflection

Read Matthew 19:13-15.

Reflect upon what it means to receive His kingdom like a child.

Respond by reaching out to children with the love of Jesus, for their hearts are moldable and hungry for love!

Pray for the children in your life to be "shiny for Jesus" just as you pray for yourself to be.

> *"In the same way, let your light shine before others,*
> *that they may see your good deeds and*
> *glorify your Father in heaven."*
> (Matthew 5:16)

Sounds of Heaven

Peals of thunder split the sky,
I sensed the presence of the Most High;

Could He be expressing displeasure,
Against evil without measure?

More atrocities mark the news,
People groping and confused;

We have sinned and gone our own way,
Oh, how we need to cry out and pray!

Overwhelmed with Your power,
Followed by a healing shower;

As rain pelted down without relief,
I felt such intense grief!

Many lost, hurting, angry souls,
Needing desperately to be made whole!

Only Jesus can deliver and restore,
He is knocking on each heart's door!

May we be His messengers!

Broken Shells

Venturing out to the beach after a night of thunder and lightning, I hoped for a short reprieve. Glimmers of light through the clouds brought some hope, but only for the moment. Soon, the persistent rain began again.

I spotted one lone woman walking briskly and I soon caught up to her. Her name was Carol, and she was enjoying the unique beauty of God's creation in spite of the rain and wind. She was also picking up shells to take home, hoping to find a sand dollar. Showing each other our shells, I told her how I used to choose only "perfect" ones, but now, I appreciate the broken ones, because of another friend with whom I had shared a special conversation on an airplane. She opened her heart and life to me revealing her disappointment and brokenness. Meeting her seemed to be divinely orchestrated. As she and I talked, I sensed she was open to hearing another woman's story. I was able to tell her the following true story from the Bible that had deeply touched my life.

Though known to be an immoral woman, she came to see Jesus while He was dining at the home of Simon, a religious leader. She lavishly loved Jesus. Through her tears, she wiped His feet, anointed them with expensive perfume and then began to kiss Him. Simon was thinking, if this man were a prophet, He would know who this woman is, who's touching Him, that she is a sinner. (Luke 7:36-50)

As I continued telling her the story, I said "We were able to see a picture of Jesus' forgiving this woman. He told Simon that even though her sins were many, they had been forgiven for she loved much." Jesus then told the woman, "Your faith has saved you, go in peace."

At that point she said strongly, "That is who Jesus is, isn't it?

I assured her that we have all experienced brokenness but He came to forgive and restore us to wholeness in Him.

We prayed together for her to experience His love in her life. Since then, she has become a dear friend. She brought me a gift, a big Styrofoam ball covered with shells.

She explained to me, "This represents how God uses you to pick up broken people and place them into His plan and purpose."

My friend Carol, the woman on the beach, was touched by this story; and you will see how she related it to life in our next story, "Healing Rain."

Personal Reflection

Read Luke 7: 36-50.

Reflect upon how this story touches you personally.

Respond by praying for someone you can share this story with as you find His hope for restoration.

Restored

Every life a grand design,
Our Creator had in mind;

Broken hearts and empty dreams,
Are part of Satan's schemes;

Countless lies that lead to pain,
Healed by His healing rain;

He alone picks up the pieces,
His gracious love never ceases;

No matter how broken,
For you He has spoken!

On the cross He carried all,
The brokenness from the fall!

He extends arms wide,
Inviting us to His side.

Healing Rain

After telling Carol the story of my friend and the broken shells, I picked up a uniquely worn and broken one.

She quickly said, "That is my life!" She began to share with me how her husband left her for another woman on Thanksgiving Day. As a single mother with two children, she sought help from a religious leader who said he couldn't help her! Obviously, she expressed deep disappointment and rejection.

That is when I shared some of my life's journey and offered to tell her a story of hope. She listened eagerly as I told her the same story I had shared with my friend about a woman in the Bible who was also feeling rejection and shame. All the time I was recounting the story we continued walking in the rain. I sensed the Lord's healing rain begin to wash over her. Finishing the woman's story from the Bible, I offered my own experience of brokenness that had led me to give my heart to Jesus to forgive me, deliver me and heal me. We connected at a deeper level as she listened intently.

I invited her to receive the gift of forgiveness through what Jesus Christ had done on the cross when He paid the penalty for our sin, experiencing, suffering and separation from His Father in heaven. Indeed, Jesus knew Carol by name and had tenderly prepared her heart.

With rain washing over us, we prayed together for her to open her heart to receive the gift of His salvation and eternal life!

Then, she exclaimed "I've been baptized with this rain!" What joy we experienced through the grace of Jesus' love!

We laughed and hugged each other. Carol was celebrating her 90-year-old mother's birthday, so I gave her a beautiful film of the life of Jesus as seen through the eyes of Mary Magdalene also a broken woman set free by Jesus!

Who would know how one broken life could mend another? Only our beautiful Savior! Jesus' broken body was given to heal ours. We in turn use our brokenness to heal another, everyone a part of God's divine masterpiece.

Personal Reflection

Read Psalm 139.

Reflect upon His intimate knowledge of every detail of your life and of those you encounter daily.

How precious to me are your thoughts, God!
How vast is the sum of them! Were I to count them,
they would outnumber the grains of sand—
when I awake, I am still with you.
(Psalm 139:17-18)

Respond by praying that you may be used as an instrument of healing and life giving hope.

Shepherd Of My Heart

Gentle rain wash over me,
Cleanse my heart so I can see;

More of You and less of me,
I surrender all to Thee;

Guide me on Your Spirit's wings,
So my heart and life sings,

Of Your majestic glory,
Truly my love story.

Renew my passionate delight,
As I gaze on You in sight...

Holy Spirit have Your way,
I'll respond to all You say.

Catching Fish

Will had his pole ready for a catch. Shrimp was his bait and he was waiting patiently. I asked him "Do you know the greatest fisherman who ever lived?"

This cute 17-year-old junior in high school was hooked.

"Who?" he asked.

"Let me tell you a story and see if you know," I responded.

He didn't have much else to do besides wait for the fish to bite, so I began. He was ready to listen.

"One day this guy told his friends to put their nets into the deep water for a catch. They had been fishing all night and had not caught anything, but because He told them to, they did! They were amazed as they caught so many fish their nets began to break! Their partners in another boat had to come help, and they filled both boats so full they began to sink.

I paused to ask Will if he knew who it was. He was not sure, until I told him,

"It was Jesus! Do you know anything about Him?"

Will told me he had gone to Catholic school, but had not been to church in a while. Continuing with the story, I explained how Simon Peter fell at Jesus feet when he saw this miracle, and told Jesus to go away from him because he was a sinful man. However, Jesus told him, "Don't be afraid; from now on you will catch men." So they left their boats and everything to follow Jesus.

Will said he did not know Jesus in a personal way, but when I asked if he wanted to, he said, "Yes!" Just then his cousin, Kate who was 13 years old came with her fishing pole, needing his help!

What a joy to explain to both of them how to receive Jesus as their Saviour who came to pay for their sins. Together we all prayed out loud to open their hearts and lives to Jesus. I was able to give them a video of the story of Jesus from the Gospel of Luke.

What an adventure to go fishing with Jesus and enlist some new young fishermen!

Personal Reflection

Read Luke 5:1-11.

Reflect on when you first encountered Jesus! Did you feel unworthy of His love? Have you made a decision to follow Him?

Respond in prayer that you will experience the joy of being a "fisher of men!" Ask Jesus, who needs to hear His story.

> *"Come, follow me," Jesus said,*
> *"and I will send you out to fish for people."*
> (Matthew 4:19)

nothing can change God's love for you!

Come Away

Come away and be with me,
There is new truth to see;

Gazing at the peaceful sea,
Is an incredible reality.

In quietness and rest is my strength,
You went the entire length;

To accomplish all,
was Your call!

My role is to abide and obey,
Trust, rest and always pray!

I give my little loaves and fish,
It is my one and only wish;

For You to bless and multiply,
is my passionate cry!

For many to be fed,
with Your heavenly bread;

Jesus, bread of life, come,
to deliver us all from...

Our brokenness and shame;
You know us all by name!

Prayed For

Have you ever felt led so strongly to pray a prayer, not knowing when or how it will come to be?

One morning, I asked the Lord God to lead me to His precious Jewish people. He has placed in my heart such a love for the chosen people of God to know Yeshua their Messiah.

They are not better than others; it is just that God wanted to demonstrate His covenant love through establishing a unique and set apart people for Himself. It all began in Genesis 12, when God called Abram.

The Lord had said to Abram,
"Go from your country, your people and
your father's household to the land I will show you.
I will make you into a great nation, and I will bless you;
I will make your name great, and you will be a blessing.
I will bless those who bless you, and whoever curses you
I will curse; and all peoples on earth
will be blessed through you."
(Genesis 12: 1-3)

God's faithfulness to His covenant people is evident all throughout history, even though He judged and punished them when they disobeyed Him and followed other gods. His promises are still true today; and one day He will completely fulfill every promise He has made.

By seeing how God honors His Holy Word, we can also trust Him to fulfill His promises to us. There will come a day when the eyes of the Jewish people will be opened to see Yeshua (Jesus is a Jew) as their Messiah. Even now, a number of Jews are coming to this revelation with many more needing still to recognize Him.

Therefore, as a Gentile who is grateful for the covenant that I have become a part of, through receiving Jesus, the Messiah, as my beloved Savior and King, I pray for the Jewish people to recognize Him as their Messiah.

Walking on the beach this morning, I met two women from

Dallas, Texas; one had a Texas star on her hat. After visiting awhile, I offered them a beautiful DVD with the story of Jesus. Debbie gladly received the gift; but Michelle, with the star, refused it. At that moment, I just knew she was Jewish.

I asked if she were, and smiling, she said, "Yes!"

"I'm so happy to meet you," I exclaimed! "I have many Jewish friends, and even attend a Jewish synagogue where I have learned so much."

She asked, "Are they Messianic Jews?"

I responded, "Yes, they have realized Yeshua (Jesus) was a Jew who came to them first, but many did not recognize Him, since He came the first time as a suffering servant (Isaiah 53). One day soon He will come as King to rule and reign eternally from Zion!" (Zechariah 9).

I was able to explain this simply to Michelle and also share a testimony of my Jewish friend who studied the New Testament and saw Jesus clearly as the Messiah, fulfilling every prophecy given. "In fact, all of His first disciples were Jews who all died martyrs' deaths after the resurrection of Jesus," I declared.

> *As for us, we cannot help speaking about*
> *what we have seen and heard.*
> (Acts 4:20)

Michelle listened closely and thanked me! As I left, I encouraged her to ask God to show her if Jesus is the Messiah; for He desires each of us to seek Him for ourselves.

> *"For I know the plans I have for you," declares the Lord, "plans*
> *to prosper you and not to harm you, plans to give you hope and a*
> *future. Then you will call on me and come and pray to me,*
> *and I will listen to you. You will seek me and find me*
> *when you seek me with all your heart."*
> (Jeremiah 29:11-13)

God gave us a heart-to-heart connection that I pray will give her a hunger to search out the truth. I trust her friend will be able to continue being a light to her and that Yeshua will reveal Himself to her.

Personal Reflection

Read Zechariah 8-12 and you will see the prophecies yet to be fulfilled.

Reflect on Isaiah 53 and what He has done to take our sins upon His own body and become the sacrificed lamb who took our place as payment for sin.

Respond in praise that Jesus came, and fulfilled the name for God, Jehovah, by revealing Himself as every "I AM," in the book of John.

God loves each of *us* as if there were only one of *us!*

Prepare the Way

Deep darkness covers the earth,
Awaiting Your holy birth;

Prophets were long ago told,
To speak out and be bold;

Calling people to follow You,
Dispelling lies by what was true;

One day a promised Savior would come,
Sent from our Father above;

So precious, humble and small,
Yet He is the Lord of all;

No one can tell the full measure,
Of this exceedingly great treasure;

In eternity we will know,
All His glory will show;

So glorious, radiant and holy,
Yet He stooped to be lowly;

He came to earth to die,
It was to purchase you and I;

His holy sacrifice fulfilled,
The wrath of God stilled;

Many voices calling, "Prepare the way,"
Behold He comes with clouds one day.

Freed Indeed

S topping in the office of the apartment complex where I lived, Jake greeted me with a sense of urgency.

"Nancy, I need to talk to you. I know you love God because you're always smiling and saying, "God bless you."

I did not really know Jake yet, other than seeing him at the front office. He was a young 22-year-old hired fairly recently right out of college.

"Okay Jake," I said smiling , "Can you take a break?" As soon as we sat down outside, he burst forth with his desperate cry for help.

Jake opened his heart and life to me confessing his addiction to alcohol, which was destroying him. Knowing his father would be devastated if he knew, he also confided in me that he was trapped in a gay lifestyle.

His shame and despair touched my heart deeply. I could identify with his addiction because of my own struggle with too much drinking in college and of having to overcome an eating disorder.

Looking straight into his hopeless eyes, I said, "Jake, God knows and He loves you. You did not know this, but I also have struggled with an addiction. Only God could have led you to open your heart to me today."

"I want to tell you a true story," I continued. "One day Jesus and His disciples crossed the Sea of Galilee. Right away, as Jesus got out of the boat, a man with evil spirits came from the tombs to meet him. This man was incapable of helping himself for he was controlled by many evil spirits until he came face-to-face with Jesus. "What do you want with me, Jesus Son of the most high God? Swear to God that you won't torture me."

Jesus then commanded the evil spirits to leave the man! Immediately, He sent them into a herd of 2,000 pigs that ran into a lake and drowned. The man was delivered and the village was in an uproar!

We can only imagine the shock and fear as the people saw the change in this man. When they came to Jesus, they saw the man who had been possessed by demons sitting there, dressed and in his right mind.

"Jake, what do you think of this story?" I asked.

"I don't know much about Jesus but I really like the way Jesus delivered the man," he responded.

"Jake, it's no accident you shared your heart with me today," I replied. "I too was in a desperate place when Jesus revealed His love and truth to me, the truth that set me free! He can deliver you also, and set you free. That is why He came, and He died on the cross to pay for all our sin and shame on the cross. Would you like to ask Him to come into your heart, forgive your sin and set you free?"

Jake followed as I led him in prayer.

"Lord Jesus, I need You. Please forgive my sin and come into my life. I want to be Your child. Thank You, Jesus, for Your promises."

Yet to all who did receive him, to those who believed in his name, he gave the right to become children of God. (John 1:12).

Jake and I hugged. He agreed to meet me at church the next day so I could introduce him to the youth leader who could help him in his new journey of faith.

Jesus knew Jake by name, just as He knew the desperate plight of the demon possessed man. That story goes on to tell us that because the people were so afraid when they saw what had happened, they began to plead with Jesus to leave their region.

As Jesus was getting into the boat, the man who had been demon-possessed begged to go with him. Jesus did not let him, but said, "Go home to your own people and tell them how much the Lord has done for you, and how he has had mercy on you." So the man went away and began to tell in the Decapolis how much Jesus had done for him. And all the people were amazed. (Mark 5:18-20).

This liberated man impacted many lives! One changed life can be used greatly by God.

*How, then, can they call on the one they have not believed in?
How can they believe in the one they have not heard? How can
they hear without someone preaching to them? And, how can
anyone preach unless they are sent? As it is written: "How
beautiful are the feet of those who bring good news."*
(Romans 10:14-15)

Personal Reflection

Read Mark 5:1-20 and imagine it as you read! How did this
man feel before and after?

Reflect upon your life and how God may want to use your
testimony to reach others!

Respond by asking God to use you as His "beautiful feet."

Freed

*Such a price indeed,
for me to be freed;*

Embracing all (my) shame;

*Jesus broke the bread,
gave His blood shed;*

*Hanging on a cross,
redeeming our loss;*

*Seeing you and me,
as His victory;*

*Can we do any less?
Than to Him say Yes!!!*

*Will you open your heart,
and begin a new start?*

Divine Interruption

S oaking in the sun and meditating on His Names, enjoying
a quiet pool...what a treat!

Suddenly, three excited junior high girls jumped in the pool
giggling and comparing their swimsuits, bodies and tans. It was
hard not to listen and notice the fun they were having and the focus they had on their looks.

I commented, "You girls are having a blast. And you are all
beautiful."

My compliment seemed to hit a sweet spot because they all
swam over to where I was sitting. As I discovered more about
them and where they went to school, I told them how they reminded me of myself in junior high. Working with teen girls for
many years, I playfully related to their interest in their looks and
assured them that God had designed them each as a masterpiece.

I had indeed hit a nerve and they seemed to want to talk. Telling them a bit of my story, being concerned about friends, boys
and image, I got stuck. My eating disorder had begun innocently
enough, trying to keep up my image, until it evolved into a serious
addiction. They listened with interest as I shared how I met had
Jesus personally through coming to a desperate place and how He
had healed me and set me free.

Pausing in my story, I asked if they knew Jesus. Jenna and
Kayla said they had gone to church before, but not now. I sensed
they wanted to talk, so I suggested,

"How about if I tell you a true story of how Jesus reached out
to a woman with His love?"

"Yes, tell us!" they responded, enthusiastically.

So I began. "One day Jesus was coming to a town with His
disciples. It was hot and He was tired. He sat down at a well while
the disciples left to get food. A woman came to draw water from
the well and Jesus asked her for a drink. Surprised, she asked Him
why He would ask her, a Samaritan woman, for a drink? (Jews did
not get along well with the Samaritans; and in that culture, men
usually did not relate to women). Jesus declared that if she knew

who was asking her, she would ask Him to give her living water. The woman asked how He could get the water because the well was deep and He didn't have anything to draw with. Then He told her that if she drank the well water she would be thirsty again, but if she drank the water that He gave her she would never be thirsty again. In fact, the water would well up within her with eternal life.

"I want this water so I don't have to keep coming here to draw water!" exclaimed the woman.

Jesus told her to go get her husband. She told him she didn't have a husband. Jesus said, "You have told the truth. You have had five husbands and the one you are now living with is not your husband."

"Sir," she presumed, "You must be a prophet. I know the promised Savior is coming and He will tell us everything."

"I am He!" Jesus proclaimed.

The woman dropped her bucket and ran to the village to tell everyone. "Come, see a man who told me everything I have done. Could He be the promised Savior?"

All the people from the village came to see Jesus, and He stayed two days teaching them. Then the people told the woman "We no longer believe just because of your testimony, for we have seen and heard this man for ourselves, and we know He is the Savior of the world."

"Girls," I asked, "What do you think of the story? Is there anything you really liked?"

Kayla said, " I like that He accepted her just the way she was!" After several other comments, I added,

"Yes, Jesus loves us unconditionally, that is what drew me to Him. He came to invite us into a relationship in which He has given His life to pay for our mistakes and sins so we can become children of God.

It was so precious to see their interest and thirst to know more of this kind of love! Jesus had opened their hearts to receive more. I explained how they could invite Him to come into their hearts, forgive their mistakes and sins, and become children of God.

I asked if they wanted to do that, and they each said, "Yes!" I prayed a simple prayer as they repeated, "Lord Jesus, I need you! Thank you that you died for me. Please come into my heart and forgive my sins and make me your daughter. Thank you for dying for me. Amen."

What a divine interruption! All the angels in heaven were rejoicing. My heart was so full of joy. Jenna, Kayla and Gina were eager to get together again to talk and share.

Only Jesus knows the hearts of every little sheep that He is seeking. He truly is the Good Shepherd who goes after the lost sheep wherever they are — even in a swimming pool. Smile.

Personal Reflection

Read John 4, the story of the Samaritan woman.

Reflect on the living water that we can drink and then share with others. Ask Jesus who would be thirsty, needing the eternal water of life, with whom you can share this story.

Respond by praying and being prepared for the divine interruptions that He may bring into your life!

Devote yourselves to prayer, being watchful and thankful.
And pray for us, that God may open a door for our message,
so that we may proclaim the mystery of Christ, for which
I am in chains. Pray that I may proclaim it clearly,
as I should. Be wise in the way you act towards outsiders;
make the most of every opportunity.
Let your conversation be always full of grace,
seasoned with salt, so that you may know how
to answer everyone.
(Colossians 4:2-6)

King Of All

You are my King of all,
I alone am so small!

Called and chosen to reign,
Because Your Cross did gain!

My rescue and freedom,
Transferred to Your Kingdom!

Adopted as daughter and bride,
To rule and reign at Your side;

You alone are holy and true!
I pledge my life again to You!

Lead me on to fulfill
All that is Your perfect will;

Let me not sink back in fear,
But launch forward in high gear.

My Father and my Friend,
I go wherever You send!

If Your presence does not go with me,
I will wait and pray until I see;

May I spread Your glory and fame,
As I lift up Your Holy Name.

Trusting fully in Jesus my King.

His Presence Goes Before Us

C oupon in hand, I headed to Dunkin' Donuts after church for an iced coffee. On a hot 89 degree afternoon that sounded good. Oh, but it seemed everyone had the same idea, so I left without the iced coffee. In a five-car line, I headed home until an ambulance siren blared behind me and I had to pull into a 7-Eleven. Well, how about an iced coffee here, I thought. What a deal, 79 cents today. I hit the jackpot.

At the coffee bar, someone else was looking for a good deal as he organized his lotto tickets. Asking what he was hoping for, he said he came in every day hoping to win. I asked if he ever did? He admitted he won very rarely, but he was hooked.

"Have you ever thought there may be a better way to have your needs provided for?" I inquired. He looked up, curiously.

I took the opportunity to ask, "May I tell you a short story?" He was listening. "One day Jesus and His followers were going through a town. There was a man sitting on the road begging, for he was blind from birth. His name was Bartimaeus. When he heard that Jesus was going by, he started to shout, 'Son of David, have mercy on me.' Well, everyone told him to be quiet! But he started shouting louder, 'Son of David, have mercy on me.'"

Jesus stopped and said, *'Bring him to me!'* They told him to cheer up because Jesus was calling for him. So he threw off his cloak and jumped to his feet as they brought him to Jesus! Jesus asked him,

'What do you want me to do for you?'

He said, *'Teacher, I want to see.'*

Jesus said, *'Go! Your faith has healed you.'* Immediately, he could see and he followed Jesus on the way. What do you think?" I asked the man at the coffee bar, "Pretty cool, right?"

Nodding with a big smile, he got the point. I suggested, "Why don't you ask Jesus for what you need. He cares for you."

The man was going to work, so I gave him a Jesus video to watch later with more amazing stories of Jesus' love and care for us to watch later. Thanking me, he left.

There happened to be another woman who had joined us at the coffee bar. With her six pack in hand, she had been listening. She began to tell me all about her situation; it was obvious she had had too much alcohol. She was very upset with her family because she was the caretaker for her 85-year-old mother, and none of her brothers cared enough to help. She hugged me several times while I listened. I tried to encourage her and offer a caring ear.

I shared Jesus' love with her and told her about how He had helped me with an addiction. It seemed as if she knew about Jesus; but at that moment, I could see she was using alcohol to deal with her frustrations.

I dared to tell her that the alcohol would not help and that it could only destroy. She had tears in her eyes as she told me that she only drinks sometimes. I told her Jesus could deliver her and heal her and I prayed for her. She hugged me again and I gave her a Jesus film to watch with her mother. As she went to check out, it was clear she was drunk and was having trouble. The girl at the check-out counter seemed to be familiar with her. She left without the six pack and I told the girls it was the best for her. All the people in line agreed.

I noticed that one of the check-out girls had an accent and I suspected it to be Russian. Wow, I had been to Russia many times to minister so I asked if she had ever heard of Jesus.

"I am Muslim," she responded.

"I am glad God has brought you here so you can discover more about Jesus!" I exclaimed, She had been listening to me and it was clear her heart had been stirred. She told me her name was Albina.

"Albina," I asserted, "Jesus loves you so much." I spoke softly telling her, "He is more than a prophet... He is God, and He has come to show us the way to Our Father in heaven." Listening so closely, she smiled. I told her I would love to give her a gift, so I ran out to my car where I had the story of Jesus through the eyes of Mary Magdalena on a DVD. This film includes all the encounters Jesus had with women and how he honors them, heals them, delivers them and respects them. She thanked me for it and gave me her phone number so we could get together.

Driving away, I had a lot of dear ones to pray for. Who could ever know the amazing encounters an iced coffee would lead to? But, isn't that His way, as He goes before us, when we are about our Savior's business to "seek and to save the lost?" We sow and water seeds that we pray will become His harvest. The seeds are precious hearts, prepared by His Spirit, who we encounter as we walk in His presence.

Personal Reflection

Read the story of Blind Bartimaeus in Mark 10:46-52.

Reflect on the question Jesus asked Bartimaeus, *"What do you want me to do for you?"*

Respond by praying that you would be filled with His Holy Spirit's presence each day. Follow His leading as you pray 2 Corinthians 2:14-17.

> *But thanks be to God, who always leads us*
> *as captives in Christ's triumphal procession*
> *and uses us to spread the aroma of the knowledge*
> *of him everywhere. For we are to God*
> *the pleasing aroma of Christ among those*
> *who are being saved and those who are perishing.*
> *To the one we are an aroma that brings death;*
> *to the other, an aroma that brings life.*
> *And who is equal to such a task?*
> *Unlike so many, we do not peddle the word of God for profit.*
> *On the contrary, in Christ we speak before God*
> *with sincerity, as those sent from God.*
> (2 Corinthians 2:14-17)

His Presence

What a privilege to carry,
His presence as emissary!

Wherever our feet may go,
Ready with His love to show;

How it may happen each day new,
Depends on His Spirit in you;

His still small voice,
Leads to a choice;

Will I let Him lead,
To meet someone's need?

Oh, for His strength and grace,
To be His hands and face;

Shining from within,
Cleansed and free from sin;

We are His sweet fragrance,
With every prayerful glance.

The Ultimate Banquet

C elebrating Memorial Weekend with new friends from Syria, India, Yemen, Turkey, Iraq, Morocco, Egypt, Lebanon, Jordan, Israel and many more countries was amazing!

The weekend was organized by dear friends with a heart to welcome immigrants. Flags from every country were displayed in a parade of nations. Beautiful cultural dress was worn by all as we celebrated our diversity together. Songs, dances and presentations were performed throughout the weekend. Undoubtedly, the highlight of the weekend was the relationships and conversations! Since I have been to many of the countries represented, I really enjoyed connecting with each new friend. Love was the bond that drew us together!

One young couple from Turkey who had two children shared some of their challenges with me. I love Turkey and have been there to minister five times. In fact, my books have been translated into the Turkish language and I have done many radio shows there; so God seemed to knit our hearts together.

At the final celebration on the last evening after our meal together, I was invited to share a story with the entire group.

"We have all enjoyed the joy of blending our cultures and rejoicing in each other's uniqueness. This, I believe, is only a foretaste of the ultimate banquet to come, " I stated.

"Jesus spoke of the kingdom of heaven being like a king who prepared a wedding banquet for his son. He sent His servants to tell everyone invited to come, that a feast was prepared and ready. Sadly, they paid no attention and went off on their own pursuits; some even mistreated and killed his servants. The King was enraged and told his servants to go out again to the streets and invite all the people they could find, both good and bad, so the wedding hall would be filled with guests.

The wedding invitation was given to all, but only those who accepted it and came wearing white wedding clothes were welcomed. The others were cast out. There was protocol for the King's wedding," I submitted.

"In the same way, we see a picture of the ultimate, eternal wedding banquet in another story found in the final book of the Bible, the book of Revelation. The white wedding garments are described in Revelation 19:6-9. The Bride has prepared her white pure robe through the precious blood of the lamb of God, Jesus, that was shed for her sins."

"We see another scene in heaven of a lamb looking as if it had been slain, standing in the center of the throne in heaven. There were many worshippers singing a new song.

And they sang a new song, saying:
You are worthy to take the scroll and to open its seals,
because you were slain, and with your blood
you purchased for God persons from every tribe and
language and people and nation.
You have made them to be a kingdom and priests to serve
our God, and they will reign on the earth."
Then I looked and heard the voice of many angels,
numbering thousands upon thousands, and ten thousand times
ten thousand. They encircled the throne
and the living creatures and the elders.
In a loud voice they were saying:
"Worthy is the Lamb, who was slain,
to receive power and wealth and wisdom and strength
and honor and glory and praise!
Then I heard every creature in heaven and on earth
and under the earth and on the sea,
and all that is in them, saying:
"To him who sits on the throne and to the Lamb be praise
and honor and glory and power, for ever and ever!"
The four living creatures said, "Amen,"
and the elders fell down and worshiped.
(Revelation 5:9-14)

I continued with my presentation, "This is God's heart for people from every tongue, tribe and nation to receive the wedding invitation with great joy. Your place has already been reserved in heaven; your place has been paid for by Jesus, the One who gave His life as payment for each person's sins. He is the Sar Shalom, the Prince of Peace, who made peace by paying for our sins on the cross and rose again to conquer sin and death."

I then invited my new international friends to receive this gift.

"Will you, my friend, come to receive this ultimate invitation today? If this is new to you simply ask and He will reveal more of Himself to you."

As I prayed a simple prayer of salvation, some precious new friends bowed their heads out of respect and some prayed along with me. Praise Jesus, my Turkish friends were among those who prayed to receive Jesus as their Savior.

I believe all the angels in heaven were rejoicing that day.

Personal Reflection

Read the parable of the wedding banquet in Matthew 22:1-14.

Reflect on the ultimate wedding banquet that is coming soon! Rejoice that you've been invited and make sure your reservation is secure

Respond by reaching out to people of different ethnicities to share the heavenly invitation. Pray for the Lord to open their hearts and minds to His truth.

> *"And this gospel of the kingdom will be preached in the whole world as a testimony to all nations, and then the end will come."*
> (Matthew 24:14)

Be Ready!

I hear the trumpet call!
Every knee will fall;

The King is coming to reign,
Jesus, who once was slain;

Purchased His Beloved Bride,
To forever rule at His side;

Rejoice and give Him glory,
As He completes His story!

Woe to those unprepared,
Was the truth not shared?

Oh, how can it be so sad?
My heart cannot be glad...

Until everyone has heard,
The Gospel, the Word;

This is our Holy Commission,
Forgive our sin of omission;

Compel us to preach,
With a passion to reach;

Giving the wedding invitation,
Without pride or hesitation;

Jesus will come sooner than we think,
Many souls hang on the brink;

Plead and persuade with zeal,
Inviting to the wedding meal!

Come Lord Jesus, ignite a fire,
Awaken us with Your desire!

Do You Know Him by Name?

God invites you into His eternal love story!

Do You Know Him by Name?

C an you even imagine that the Creator of the Universe, Our God, wants us to know Him?

This understanding has rocked my world. You see, not only does He know us by name, and have a plan, purpose and destiny for us; but He invites us into an intimate relationship with Him. He does this by revealing Himself to us through His many names.

I discovered this through Dr. Bill Bright, the founder of Campus Crusade for Christ, who was such a humble, godly servant of the Lord and also a spiritual father to me. He always impressed upon his staff that the attributes of God are the most important things we could learn or teach another because how we view God affects every aspect of our lives.

The names of God reveal His character, His nature, His purposes and His commitments to us. I can guarantee that the more we know about Him, the more we will love and trust Him. He wants us to pursue Him, seek after Him and draw close to His heart.

> *Give praise to the Lord, proclaim his name;*
> *Look to the Lord and his strength;*
> *seek his face always.*
> (Psalm 105:1a, 3-4)

His names are revealed throughout the Bible as He interacts with His people and shows His commitment and care for them. His covenant love for them is demonstrated over and over again!

> *Lord, our Lord, how majestic is your name in all the earth!*
> (Psalm 8:9)

Whatever our needs and struggles, He is there to help us. I have found comfort and strength during a time of sorrow and suffering through meditating on one of His names!

My mother had Alzheimer's for 10 years. It was a painful, sad experience for our family to watch her go through this. One day when I was feeling so sad, I read in the Bible about the Lord God Almighty as our shepherd (Jehovah Rohi).

> *He tends his flock like a shepherd:*
> *He gathers the lambs in his arms*
> *and carries them close to his heart;*
> *He gently leads those that have young.*
> (Isaiah 40:11)

It was as if I saw the Lord in such a tender way, lifting my helpless mother in His arms and carrying her close to His heart. I found a picture that depicted this and had it framed with this Scripture to place above her bed in the nursing home. It gave me peace and comfort every time I went to see her, and when it came time for her to go to heaven I relied upon El Olam, the eternal God.

As we see in the Book of Ruth...

> *May the Lord repay you for what you have done.*
> *May you be richly rewarded by the Lord, the God of Israel,*
> *under whose wings you have come to take refuge.*
> (Ruth 2:12)

So you will see, my friend, that

> *The name of the Lord is a fortified tower;*
> *the righteous run to it and are safe.*
> (Proverbs 18:10)

As you focus on some of His names, you will experience your trust growing and your love for the Lord increasing. You will become more intimately acquainted with His ways and His heart!

> *Those who know your name trust in you,*
> *for you, Lord, have never forsaken those who seek you.*
> (Psalm 9:10)

My Elohim

My Elohim of greatest esteem

I render my praise to the Ancient of Days

Beginning and End, Alpha and Omega

You alone transcend all that is temporal.

I lift up my heart to You, unshakable and true.

May I perceive Your majesty, open my eyes to see

The glory and wonder of Your being

To experience and know without seeing.

I fall on my knees with earnest pleas.

You are my expectation, in eager anticipation...

Captivate my imagination with fresh invigoration!

Soaring with You in faith and joy!

God's love is unending!

Worthy of Our Trust

You can trust God only to the extent that you know Him. The more you look through the prism of God's glorious names, the more you will see His majestic character. Each name reveals God's magnificent qualities, His steadfast promises, and a history of His marvelous faithfulness.

> *Praise your name for your unfailing love and*
> *your faithfulness, for you have so exalted your*
> *solemn decree that it surpasses your fame.*
> (Psalm 138:2)

His Name

> *Therefore God exalted him to the highest place*
> *and gave him the name that is above every name,*
> *that at the name of Jesus every knee should bow,*
> *in heaven and on earth and under the earth,*
> *and every tongue acknowledge that Jesus Christ is Lord,*
> *to the glory of God the Father.*
> (Philippians 2:9-11)

ALL *things* are possible with *God*

Names and Titles of Jesus

Jesus reveals Himself...

I Am the Bread of Life (John 6:35) - satisfying love
I Am the Light of the World (John 8:12) - revealing love
I Am from Above (John 8:23) - supernatural love
I Am the Gate (John 10:7) - pursuing love
I Am the Door (John 10:9) - liberating love
I Am the Good Shepherd (John 10:11) - fatherly love
I Am the Son of God (John 10:36) - passionate love
I Am the Resurrection and the Life (John 11:25) -
    overcoming love
I Am the Way, the Truth and the Life (John 14:6) -
    all sufficient love
I Am the True Vine (John 15:1) - intimate love

Beautiful You Are

Beloved body of Christ,
Purchased and prized;

Beautiful Shepherd King
Praises to proclaim and sing,

Beautiful promises to hold,
Declared and told;

Beautiful Beloved Bride,
Reigning at His side;

Beautiful feet to preach,
Many lost to reach;

Beautiful, no two the same,
He Knows You by Name.

ᴄ𝒩ames of 𝒥esus

He is my **Wonderful Counselor** in times of aloneness or uncertainty.

He is my **Mighty God** in times of weakness or temptation.

He is my **Everlasting Father** when friends and family fail us.

He is my **Prince of Peace** when feeling stressed, worried or confused.

> *For to us a child is born, to us a son is given,*
> *and the government will be on his shoulders.*
> *And he will be called Wonderful Counselor,*
> *Mighty God, Everlasting Father, Prince of Peace.*
> (Isaiah 9:6)

He is my **Creator** and my **Maker** (Colossians 1:15, 16)

He is my **Sin Bearer**, the **Lamb of God**, when feeling condemnation or guilt. (John 1:29, Revelation 5:12)

He is my **Captain of Salvation** (Hebrews 2:10)

He is my **Redeemer** and **Messiah** (Titus 6:35, Jeremiah 50:34a)

He is my **Bread of Life** who satisfies my spiritual hunger (John 6:35)

He is my **Spirit of Truth and Freedom** when needing direction and deliverance from our sin and bondage (John 14:6)

He is my **True Vine**, the source of life (John 15:5)

He is my **Secure Foundation,** my **Cornerstone** (2 Peter 2:6)

He is my **Sanctifier** the **Holy One** (1 Corinthians 1:2)

He is my **Bridegroom,** my **Beloved** companion when needing to feel cherished (Ephesians 5:25-27 ; Revelation 19:7)

He is my **Bright Morning Star** when I need focus for darkness and difficulty (Revelation 22:16)

He is my **Lord of Lords** and **King of Kings** (Philippians 2:9-11)

He is my **High Priest**, my **Intercessor** (Hebrews 7:24-26)

He is my **Leader,** my **Light of the World** who shows me my mission and destiny (John 8:12)

He is my **Resurrection and Life** (John 11:25)

He is my **Hope of Glory** when the world seeks to bring hopelessness and despair (Colossians 1:27-28)

Treasure Exchanged

Costly jewel of a King,
Makes my soul sing!

Precious One from heaven sent,
Path of humility He went;

Taking on our humanity,
To open the gate to eternity!

Healings and forgiveness He brought
Many lost sheep He sought!

He became the spotless Lamb,
Replacing Abraham's ram;

You, my friend, are His treasure,
Created for His delight and pleasure;

For you know that it was not with
perishable things such as silver or gold
that you were redeemed from the empty
way of life handed down from your
forefathers, but with the precious blood
of Christ, a lamb without blemish or defect.
He was chosen before the creation of the
world, but was revealed in these last times
for your sake.
Through him you believe in God,
who raised him from the dead and glorified him,
and so your faith and hope are in God...
(1 Peter 1:18-21)

He Calls You by Name

God invites you into His eternal love story!

𝓗𝑒 𝓒𝑎𝑙𝑙𝑠 𝓨𝑜𝑢 𝑏𝑦 𝓝𝑎𝑚𝑒

For many years I knew a lot about God and believed in Him with all my heart. I wanted to please Him and honor Him with my life. So I tried very hard to be a good person, to love other people and to have high morals. In fact, on the outside I looked "put together" having lots of friends, faith and a good family; but inside, I knew my own selfishness, pride and insecurity. Trying to overcome these feelings through popularity and success led me plummet into an eating disorder. No one knew my secret struggle, as I battled this addiction. In fact, I was voted the "friendliest girl in high school." I was a cheerleader, on the drama team, on the student council and a leader in my youth group. You get the picture, a nice "put together package on the outside."

College life only increased the struggle because of all the pressure, parties and boys. One Sunday I found myself in church; I was so depressed with my life and feeling helpless to overcome my eating disorder, drinking and compromising my values.

Crying out to God, I prayed a desperate prayer. "Lord, I need You to help me. If You are God and I know You are, please deliver me. If not I'm not coming back here."

At that life-defining moment, I heard a voice in my spirit ask "Nancy, do you know Me?"

Clearly I knew it was Jesus, asking me. "Lord," I responded in my heart, "I know about You, but I can't be a hypocrite anymore. I don't know You. Show me who You are and how You can heal me."

I left church that day with a sense of expectancy. Little did I know how quickly the Lord would answer. It was as if He had been waiting for me to get to the end of my own self efforts.

Within a few days my girlfriend invited me to a popcorn party on relationships. Surprisingly I learned about three types of love, *Eros*, romantic love, *Phileo*, friendship love and *Agape*, God's unconditional love.

It was as if a light came on in my heart and I understood God's personal love for me, as shown through Jesus. Distinctly, I realized I could never do enough to earn "unconditional love" because it is a gift. But God demonstrates His great love for us, *while we were yet sinners, Christ died for us.* (Romans 5:8) *For it is by grace you have been saved, through faith—and this is not from yourselves, it is the gift of God—not by works, so that no one can boast* (Ephesians 2:8- 9)

Grasping this incredible love that God had for me and His desire to have an intimate relationship with me overwhelmed me. Tears began to flow down my cheeks as I considered this invitation to receive His undeserved gift of grace and forgiveness.

*Yet to all who did receive him, to those who believed in his name, he gave the right to become children of Go*d— (John 1:12)

Suddenly I got it! The Big picture! God's eternal love story had to involve His pursuing each one of us so that we could whole heartedly respond by surrendering our hearts and lives to Him.

Here I am! I stand at the door and knock. If anyone hears my voice and opens the door, I will come in and eat with that person, and they with me. (Revelation 3:20)

Never have I experienced a more powerful encounter with God that has changed my entire life!

My friend led me in a simple prayer. "Jesus, I want to know You. Thank You for dying on the cross for my sins. I open the door of my life and receive You as my Savior and Lord. Thank You for forgiving my sins and giving me eternal life. Take control of my life. Make me the kind of person You want me to be."

Jesus was so near and real to me, at that moment. I felt as if chains were broken and a new freedom flowed into my heart. "God loves me! He knows me! He accepts me! I'm forgiven!"

I could hardly wait to tell my friends and family and everyone. Who could possibly resist such love, if they truly understood the offer. All my problems and struggles suddenly seemed so small in light of the Creator of ALL who cared about me and all of us!

My friend, you too are dearly loved by God and He desires for you also to know Him as Your Savior, Father and Friend. You may not understand everything, neither did I, but He does. He draws our hearts to begin an eternal relationship as His son or daughter.

Simply ask Him now.

"Lord Jesus, reveal to me who You are and how You gave Your life for me! Come into my heart, cleanse me from my sin, and show me Your plan for my life now and forever!"

My dear friend, if you have expressed this prayer to God, He has heard and answered you. You have begun an awesome journey to know the One who has created you and called you by name.

Called by Name

"Nancy do you know Me?"
I heard Him ask so sweetly;

Not knowing where I was going,
In His grace, He was showing...

Reaching up, I took His hand,
As I stood up to stand;

"Lord, I will wait for You to show,"
in my tears I longed to know;

Leaving church with a prayer,
And a heartfelt dare;

Jesus heard my plea,
And He set me free!

Receiving His gift of grace,
I saw His loving face!

My journey was begun,
Now I'm learning to run...

He sets my pace,
As I run His race.

Calling me by name,
I will never be the same!

His Call Goes To All

G od loves me?" asked Katrina, an amazed young high school student in Moscow, Russia. Her puzzled look made me smile with joy. After 70 years of communism and socialism, the wall had fallen as winds of freedom blew. Only God knows how many heartfelt prayers were lifted up around the world for this miracle to occur.

You see, after Jesus touched my heart with His love and gift of forgiveness and healing, I was called to share His love to young people all over the world. Eventually I became the Associate National Director of Cru High School ministry, and then had the privilege to help launch and lead our International Ministry.

How exciting it was to be led by Jesus to each location He opened for us to take teams of high school students to reach other students with this life changing message of God's love and salvation.

What a phenomenal moment in HIStory...to seize this open door with such spiritual hunger among these precious teenagers and people everywhere in Russia. On subways people would literally rush at us to grab the Bibles we freely offered. We laughed with delight and called it the "Subway Spiritual Surge!"

Teachers were so grateful for us coming with our teams. One Principal, Maria, was so overjoyed at the gift we gave of Bibles for everyone that she hugged Chuck, our National Director, so tightly that she cracked his rib...a painful but powerful gift of gratitude never to be forgotten by Chuck.

One special high school assembly I will never forget. I had the privilege of presenting the message of Jesus' life, death and resurrection as I shared the clear evidence and how it had radically gang and the leader's name was Sergei. As I gave the invitation to receive God's gift of forgiveness and eternal life by becoming a child of God, it seemed as if the entire school stood to pray with me to receive Jesus as their Lord and Savior. Only Jesus knows the heart of each person.

Later Sergei shared, "Nancy my gang and I had been planning to rob the American students, but I decided that night to first read the book given to all the students by Josh McDowell, *More than a Carpenter.*" Josh shares his journey of investigating the claims of Jesus Christ and the compelling evidence for the resurrection, along with his own broken childhood. After researching the facts, Josh became convinced that Jesus was God, and had a radical transformation as he chose to receive Jesus as His Lord and Savior.

Sergei was so impacted that he also gave his heart to Jesus. A crime was diverted, and a radical follower of Jesus began his new life as a young leader in Moscow, eventually becoming a pastor.

Katrina was also one of the many precious students who heard Jesus call her by name personally and responded by accepting the invitation.

> *Yet to all who did receive him, to those who believed in his*
> *name, he gave the right to become children of God.*
> (John 1:12)

All they had to do was to trust (believe in) Him to save them.

My friend, He knows each of us by name. Have you heard Him call your name?

Personal Reflection

Read John 20, one of the eyewitness accounts of Jesus' resurrection. Marvel and consider the evidence of **The Most Significant** miracle that proves the Deity of Jesus Christ! Please notice in particular, Mary Magdalene's encounter with Jesus after she sees HIM ALIVE!

Reflect upon Mary, who had been delivered of seven demons by Jesus and became His devoted follower. She stood with his mother at the foot of the cross as they watched His suffer ing death. We can only imagine her anguish and sorrow. Jesus was her hope giver, her life restorer, her Lord and Savior. Who could imagine that she would be the first one He appeared to after He rose from the dead! How would this encounter with the resurrected Jesus change her life forever?

Respond with joy that Jesus chose Mary to declare the great news, *"Go to my brothers and tell them, I am ascending to my Father and your Father, to my God and your God."*

Mary ran to announce the Good News, *"I have seen the Lord."* (John 20:18). She had been a broken, troubled and lost woman possessed by demons who now was the first messenger of the resurrected Jesus!

Just as Sergei became convinced of the resurrection of Jesus, his life was changed forever just as Mary's did. He began to share the Good News. How about you my friend? Have you investigated the evidence of the resurrection of Jesus Christ?

Our eternal destiny hinges on this fact... because Jesus rose from the dead we also can live forever.

"I am the resurrection and the life.
The one who believes in me will live, even though they die."
(John 11:25)

He Called Her by Name

What grief and sorrow,
filled her tomorrow;

She knew Him as deliverer,
became His follower;

Pure, unbridled dedication,
Full of awe and adoration;

Following Him to the cross,
Grieving her unimaginable loss;

Anointing His body for the grave,
Her own life He came to save;

She came early the third day,
Finding the stone rolled away;

Tears blinded her weary eyes,
Amidst her sorrowful cries;

She beheld two angels in white,
A shocking glorious sight!

"They have taken my Lord away,"
Grieving in her dismay;

"Woman, why are you weeping?
Whom are you seeking?"

She quickly turned around,
Hearing this tender sound;

"Mary," Jesus called her name,
She would never by the same!

"I HAVE SEEN THE LORD!"

He Leads You by Name

God invites you into His eternal love story!

He Leads You by Name

O pening my heart to receive this amazing gift of forgiveness, grace and unconditional love changed my entire perspective on life.

It was as if God opened my eyes to see how He had created me for a special purpose. I began to see Him as my loving Father who had actually formed me and designed me in my mother's womb intentionally.

For you created my inmost being; you knit me together in my mother's womb. I praise you because I am fearfully and wonderfully made; your works are wonderful, I know that full well. My frame was not hidden from you when I was made in the secret place, when I was woven together in the depths of the earth. Your eyes saw my unformed body; all the days ordained for me were written in your book before one of them came to be.
(Psalms 139:13-16)

Previously, the Bible had been a holy book to me; but I had not experienced the intimate love of God when I read it. Now, the presence and power of God as revealed in Jesus captured my heart. I will never forget reading the book of Isaiah, the prophet. As God's child it became clear to me that our heavenly Father knows each of His children by name and calls us to Him personally.

"I, the Lord, have called you in righteousness; I will take hold of your hand." (Isaiah 42:6a) *"See, the former things have taken place, and new things I declare; before they spring into being I announce them to you."* (Isaiah 42:9)

Never before had I known such an intimate relationship with God, my Creator. It was as if He was assuring me that He was holding my hand; and He wanted me to let go of my past mistakes and embrace my new identity, as His Beloved daughter.

"This is what the Lord says... He who formed you. Fear not, for I have redeemed you: I have summoned you by name. You are mine." (Isaiah 43:1) *Before I was born the Lord called me; from my mother's womb he has spoken my name.* (Isaiah 49:1)

What tender, yet powerful love God had for me to rescue me from my sin and shame by paying for it Himself. When Jesus Christ hung on the cross to redeem me, He purchased me with His precious blood. (Redeem means to buy back.)

Our loving Father sent His own Son to save us from the penalty of sin and also to show us His ways. He cares for us as a Shepherd cares for His sheep. Jesus is our Good Shepherd.

"The gatekeeper opens the gate for him, and the sheep listen to his voice. He calls his own sheep by name and leads them out. When he has brought out all his own, he goes on ahead of them, and his sheep follow him because they know his voice."
(John 10:3-4)

"I am the good shepherd; I know my sheep and my sheep know me. Just as the Father knows me and I know the Father and I lay down my life for the sheep." (John 10:14-15)

"My sheep listen to my voice; I know them, and they follow me." (John 10:27)

These verses all came alive for me while I was in Slovakia. One day in a quaint little town, there was a shepherd walking with his flock of sheep. It was such a delight to see how they followed him. Excited to pet them, I ran over and only to see them run away from me while making noises. BAH. Only the shepherd was left.

"Don't worry," he reassured me, and then he held his hand out and called them each by name. Immediately they came, and as long as he was by their side, they allowed me to pet them.

How similar it is with Lord Jesus who taught us that we are safe with Him and are guided by Him. Each one of us, as one of His sheep, is unique to Him and is protected from evil. The beautiful picture in Psalm 23 that describes this secure relationship.

The Lord is my shepherd, I lack nothing.
He makes me lie down in green pastures
He leads me beside quiet waters,
He refreshes my soul.
He guides me along the right paths
for His name's sake.
(Psalm 23:1-3)

167

Not only does He care for each sheep by name, but He is passionate about finding the lost sheep. My friend and I were leading a High School missions team in Bulgaria and our trip to the quaint village was prompted by His love. One of our translators, who just received Jesus as her Savior, was very concerned about her mother, who was dying, and did not know Jesus.

As we came to her home, the mother way lying on the bed with little life left. I took my anointing oil and we prayed over her for God's Spirit to revive and rescue her from death without knowing Jesus.

Supernaturally she sat up, fully conscious, and able to talk. Her precious daughter shared the gospel, she had just come to know, and her beloved mother received Jesus as her Lord and Savior. Three days later she went to heaven to be with Jesus forever.

> *And this is the testimony: God has given us eternal life,*
> *and this life is in his Son. Whoever has the Son has life;*
> *whoever does not have the Son of God does not have life.*
> (1 John 5:11-12)

Jesus desires that none should perish, but for everyone to come to repentenance. (2 Peter 3:9)

One day Jesus was eating and sharing with tax collectors and sinners but the religious leaders were disturbed. He told them a story and asked them, "Who among you, if you had 100 sheep and lost one would not leave the 99 to go after the lost sheep? And when you find the sheep wouldn't you rejoice?"

Just as a good shepherd seeks his lost sheep, so does Jesus!

> *"I tell you that in the same way there will be more rejoicing*
> *in heaven over one sinner who repents than over*
> *ninety-nine righteous persons who do not need to repent."*
> (Luke 15:7)

Personal Reflection

Read Psalm 23 and personalize it for your life! Let it grip you with the tender love of Our Shepherd who calls His sheep by name.

Reflect on the parable of the lost sheep in Luke 15:1-7. What do you see in the heart of Jesus, Our Good Shepherd?

Respond Are you one of the lost sheep that Jesus is seeking? You can come to your Good Shepherd today as I did as a 19-year-old college freshman.

Whether you have just recently received Jesus or have known Him for awhile, He is the author of your story. It is a powerful witness to others who are in process of discovering a personal relationship with God.

Pray as you prepare your personal testimony.

1. Describe what your life was like before you received Jesus as your Savior and Lord.

2. How and when did you receive Jesus?

3. What difference or changes has Jesus made in your life?

Pray about who you may share your story with...it can have a powerful impact as you reach out to others,

They triumphed over him
by the blood of the Lamb
and by the word of their testimony;
they did not love their lives so much
as to shrink from death.
(Revelation 12:11)

My Beloved King

I approach You as Your Queen,
Your glory, no eye has seen.

And yet, You beckon me to come,
Never mind where I've come from;

My heart has been captivated.
Your regal love radiated;

Drawing me to daring grace.
As I seek You face-to-face.

I am Yours, You are mine.
All of me to intertwine;

No longer my own.
May Your Glory be shown.

Touching Your scepter's tip.
Embraced by Your graceful grip.

"What is it You desire?"
A heart set on fire.

Fulfilling Your will.
As I remain still...

You will accomplish all.
Following Your holy call!

May I be bold!
Your story told!

May the whole world make known.
Your eternal glory shown!

Embracing Your favor.
"For such a time as this."

He Leads All by Name

H ave you ever been overwhelmed with the magnitude of our universe? Learning about the vastness of the galaxies and the number of stars can be mind-blowing.

Yet nothing compares to gazing up at the stars on a clear night in the mountains in Chile. My treasured friend Lisa and I had just spoken to a huge conference in Chile for teenagers eager to learn more about Jesus.

God's heart for this generation of young people beats in my heart. I believe that He, who holds the stars, holds each of our hearts, especially the youth. I told them stories from the Bible about young people who had been used mightily in their generation...David, Mary, Daniel, Esther His first disciples Timothy, etc.

Lift up your eyes and look to the heavens:
Who created all these?
He who brings out the starry host one by one
and calls forth each of them by name.
Because of his great power and mighty strength,
not one of them is missing.
(Isaiah 40:26)

Just think, the Creator God who calls the stars by name, is also our heavenly Father, who calls each one of us by name as we embrace His gift of salvation through Jesus!

"Who has done this and carried it through,
calling forth the generations from the beginning?
I, the Lord—with the first of them
and with the last—I am He."
(Isaiah 41:4)

Not only does He know everyone of us by name, but He also leads each generation. He looks for those whose hearts are fully His. This has a mighty purpose for our generation!

For the eyes of the Lord range throughout the earth
to strengthen those whose hearts are fully committed to him.
(2 Chronicles 16:9a)

Many students in Chile gave their lives to Jesus that night and waited to talk to me personally after hearing His Word. He had prepared them to follow Him and to believe Him for their generation.

Such is the generation of those who seek him,
who seek your face, God of Jacob.
(Psalm 24:6)

Personal Reflection

Read Psalm 110:3. *Your troops will be willing on your day of battle. Arrayed in holy splendor, your young men will come to you like dew from the morning's womb.*

Jeremiah 32:17 *Ah, Sovereign Lord, you have made the heavens and the earth by your great power and outstretched arm. Nothing is too hard for you.*

Reflect Considering the magnitude of the One who is calling each of us causes us to make choices...

Will you believe that He loves you no matter what your life has been like up until now?

Will you be His messenger to connect this generation with their Creator as He completes His Eternal Love Story?

Respond Join me in inviting Him to give you His vision for your life and the fulfillment of His purposes in our generation.

Great is the Lord and most worthy of praise;
his greatness no one can fathom.
One generation commends your works to another;
they tell of your mighty acts.
(Psalm 145:3-4)

New Vision

*My King of Glory
is writing His Story (Isaiah 6:3-8)*

*His promises are true,
every day they are new (Hebrews 10:23)*

*New truth to be revealed,
His Holy Spirit has sealed! (John 3:34)*

*New faith to believe
and humbly receive (Hebrews 10:35-38)*

*All Jesus has obtained
by His blood we've gained (1 Peter 2:9-10)*

*New freedom to be secure,
our worth is sure! (Galatians 4:6-7)*

*New attention to His voice,
waiting for His choice (Isaiah 30:15-21)*

*New enterprises for our King
diminish any lesser thing. (Isaiah 49)*

*His glory is our goal
for every lost soul. (2 Peter 3:9)*

*New position for the bride,
conquering at His side. (Revelation 19)*

*New Jerusalem to see,
our glorious destiny!
He will make all things new,
Seated on His throne - Faithful and True. (Revelation 21)*

He Writes Your Story

God invites you into His eternal love story!

For His Glory

A ll the days ordained for me were written in Your book before one of them came to be. (Psalm 139:16)

Wow! One day this scripture leaped off the page. As an author, I thought "How amazing that God has written a book about my life..and He knows each chapter before I even can imagine!"

"Lord," I asked, "What's next?" Hoping for a sneak preview. Actually, I think He knows we can only handle today, with all its unique challenges, joys and sorrows.

How comforting and exciting it is to know that the God who created you and me, knit us individually in our mothers' wombs. He has a plan and a purpose for each of our lives. The more we get to know Him, the more we feel secure in this truth. His Word, the Bible, is full of precious promises. *"Can a mother forget the baby at her breast and have no compassion on the child she has born? Though she may forget, I will not forget you! See, I have engraved you on the palms of my hands; your walls are ever before me."* (Isaiah 49:15-16) I am confident that *"The LORD will work out his plans for my life."* (Psalm 138:8a NLT)

With this understanding, I've lived in anticipation of the future God has planned for me. Sometimes the path is clear and smooth, at other times, only the next step is apparent. Not to forget, there are also many divine interruptions.

My mission to Egypt was off the charts amazing! Speaking to many people of all ages and backgrounds, training in Bible Storytelling, serving refugees, along with seeing pyramids and riding camels were just some of my joy- filled adventures.

However, during the last few days, my stomach began to swell. I immediately thought that I must have a parasite from some unusual food I had eaten.

My eleven-hour flight home took some perseverance as I was experiencing not only stomach pain but also the pain of a cracked rib from a camel ride. Mohammed Jesus, the young guide, had decided to hoist me up on the camel himself. Instantly I heard the crack in my rib and felt the pain. It was worth it though because I not only enjoyed the ride, but I delighted in the special connection

God gave me to be able to share His Son, Jesus, with Mohammed Jesus! I told him how special his name was; it began with Mohammed and ended with Jesus, the Way to God! He smiled as I shared the beautiful story of Jesus and explained how He had claimed to be more than a prophet, but actually God in the flesh and the way to heaven.

Once home in the United States, after realizing the problem wasn't going away, I went to the emergency room for an x-ray, thinking everything could be taken care of simply. To my shock, I was admitted into the hospital and told that there were some serious concerns. This began a series of tests which led to a diagnosis of Stage 4 ovarian cancer. "How can this be, Lord?" I asked, as I struggled to grasp the seriousness of my prognosis.

Soon I was told that I had to have radical surgery to remove all of the cancer. The next morning I prayed, "Lord Jesus, You know all that is going on in my body, and I know You love me and care for me, Your beloved daughter! I've surrendered my entire life to You so You can choose to have me with You soon or keep me alive on this earth...but if I were you, I would have me live to declare Your Glory. And I know You are a healer! I love to tell Your miracle stories all over the world. You are the same God today. How about a new miracle with me in it, and You as My Healer?"

He reminded me of the story of Lazarus who was very sick. Jesus was a close friend of Lazarus and had spent a lot of time with him and his sisters, Mary, and Martha in their home. So the sisters sent word to Jesus saying, *"Lord, the one you love is sick" When Jesus heard this, He said, "This sickness will not end in death. No, it is for God's glory so that God's Son may be glorified through it."* (John 11:4) I was comforted that Jesus said this sickness would not end in death... but I also know the end of the story. When Jesus finally did go to Lazarus, he had already been in the grave for four days.

Mary and Martha were in mourning and did not understand why Jesus had waited to come. Both expressing the same frustration, Martha cried "Lord, if you had been here, my brother would not have died." Jesus was deeply moved and wept at the grave but the story was not over. Jesus commanded that the stone be taken

177

away and made a bold proclamation. *"Did I not tell you that if you believe, you will see the Glory of God?"* Jesus called out in a loud voice, *"Lazarus, come out!"* The dead man came forth, wrapped in linen and Jesus declared, *"Take off the grave clothes and let him live."*

This amazing miracle was preparing me for my journey of faith. I realized that Jesus has a purpose in every healing miracle, He reveals who He is! As He told Martha, *"I am the resurrection and the life; he who believes in Me will live even if he dies."* (John 11:25)

However, at the same time, I was contemplating the story, I prayed, "Jesus, please don't wait to bring me back to life after I die. Will you please heal me as a testimony to Your desire to heal today just as You did while You were on earth?"

How precious it was of Jesus to bear our sin and sickness upon His own body when He died on the cross. *"Surely he took up our pain and bore our suffering, yet we considered him punished by God, stricken by him, and afflicted. But he was pierced for our transgressions, he was crushed for our iniquities; the punishment that brought us peace was on him, and by his wounds we are healed."* (Isaiah 53:4-5)

Throughout the Bible we can find many promises of healing. Jesus healed all who asked Him and commended them for their faith. He even called and commissioned His first disciples and gave them authority over sickness and evil spirits. *Jesus called his twelve disciples to him and gave them authority to drive out impure spirits and to heal every disease and sickness.* (Matthew 10:1) He told them, *"As you go, proclaim this message: 'The kingdom of heaven has come near.' Heal the sick, raise the dead, cleanse those who have leprosy, drive out demons. Freely you have received; freely give."* (Matthew 10:7-8)

Friends all over the world joined me in **believing prayer** as we stood together on the promises of God. I am forever grateful to Jesus, who was teaching all of us how to pray as well as praying for me, since He "ever lives to intercede for us" (Hebrews 7:25) I am also forever grateful for each precious friend, who loved, prayed and supported me.

One morning as I had communion with the Lord, He reminded me of His precious Covenant with me and how He has carried me through this season of my life.

My Covenant Keeper

Oh, how awesome You are.
Whether I am near or far;

Purchased at such a high cost,
To rescue and claim the lost;

Once rescued, I became Your Bride,
To forever abide at Your side;

Covenant so secure and true,
Everyday flows mercy, so new!

You clothed me in pure white.
Oh, what a glorious sight!

No weapon can prevail,
You never will fail!

I am Yours, You are mine,
Eternally with You, I'll shine!

Your Beloved Bride,
Nancy

As I prepared for surgery, that day, the peace of God covered me like a warm blanket over my heart and mind! What a joy it was to have some dear "ministering angels" come with me to the hospital to pray during the surgery. There were also so many other friends who came to pray and encourage me during my seven-day stay. My precious nurses and doctors were such a gift, too, as they provided loving care. Each one heard about Jesus' love for him or her, and I prayed with several to receive Jesus' love and forgiveness.

Three days after the surgery, my wonderfully skilled doctor came in with the results and reported, "Nancy, all the cancer has been removed and none was found to have spread to any lymph nodes or other organs." Hallelujah! I was overjoyed and filled with awe and praise for God's love and faithfulness to me! "Doctor, the Lord gave us a miracle!" he smiled and said "Yes, He did!"

You see, before the surgery I met with him to explain I was choosing not to have chemotherapy. He was not pleased about my decision. I then explained, "You must know Doctor that I also have another doctor...He is the Great Physician...His name is Jesus! I have prayed and asked His counsel. He has clearly led me this way...to believe Him to heal me supernaturally."

I am still walking my journey of faith, as I continue to practice new healthy nutrition and natural methods along with standing on God's Word, believing the Lord for no further occurrence of cancer to appear.

Whatever the future holds, I know my God is with me to heal and restore me! He is a mountain-moving God who delights in our small mustard seed faith. *"Truly I tell you, if you have faith as small as a mustard seed, you can say to this mountain, 'Move from here to there,' and it will move. Nothing will be impossible for you."* (Matthew17:20)

No sickness or struggle you may face is hidden from our compassionate Savior, Lord and Almighty God! He holds your future in His hands and beckons you to trust and believe Him as Your healer; Jehovah Rophe (the God who heals) is His name.

And He said, "If you listen carefully to the Lord your God and do what is right in his eyes, if you pay attention to his commands and keep all his decrees, I will not bring on you any of the diseases I brought on the Egyptians, for I am the Lord, who heals you." (Exodus 15:26) *He sent out his word and healed them; He rescued them from the grave.* (Psalm 107:20)

The beautiful truth is that He has given us divine revelation to cling to in our time of trouble. His Word and His promises will strengthen us to believe that He is writing our story "for His glory"!

What a privilege I now have to tell of His marvelous miracle of healing in my life! Yes friend, you too have a testimony of how He has faithfully worked in your life to mold and shape you through each season of your journey!

> *Praise the Lord, my soul; all my inmost being,*
> *praise his holy name.*
> *Praise the Lord, my soul, and forget not all his benefits—*
> *who forgives all your sins and heals all your diseases.*
> (Psalm 103:1-3)

Personal Reflection

Read John 11:1-46 the story of Lazarus.

Reflect on Jesus' response to Lazarus' sickness and His delay to go immediately to heal him.

Are you experiencing some challenge, sickness or struggle that is causing you to ask, *"Where are you, God?"*

Respond by remembering and meditating on His faithful love that bore our sin and sickness on the cross.

> *Surely he took up our pain and bore our suffering,*
> *yet we considered him punished by God,*
> *stricken by him, and afflicted.*
> *But he was pierced for our transgressions,*
> *He was crushed for our iniquities;*
> *the punishment that brought us peace was on Him,*
> *and by His wounds we are healed.*
> (Isaiah 53:4-5)

Receive and believe these promises found in Psalm 30:1,2; Psalm 29:11; Psalm 41:2,3; Psalm 43:5; Psalm 118:17; Psalm 147:3; Psalm 103; Psalm 91; Psalm 107:20.

My Miracle Maker

My heart is in awe of You!
Ever faithful loving Lord so true!

You amaze me with Your grace,
Through each season in my race;

Overwhelmed with Your care,
Answering my every prayer!

My affection is set ablaze.
My devotion is filled with praise!

You possess my heart and soul,
I want to know You to the full!

I have seen Your glory,
In our love story!

Your Beloved Bride,
Nancy

Ah, Sovereign Lord, you have made the heavens and the
earth by your great power and outstretched arm.
Nothing is too hard for You. I am the Lord, the God of
all mankind. Is anything too hard for me?
(Jeremiah 32:17 and 27)

P.S. My spiritual son, James, in Uganda has put my poem
to music along with another musician in the United States.
Soon we will praise Him even more vibrantly as a further
faith inspiring testimony!

Your Story Reflects His Glory

Who could ever imagine that each of us would be a part of God's grand eternal story? How valuable each of us is...unique and precious.

"Indeed, the very hairs of your head are all numbered.
Don't be afraid; you are worth more than many sparrows."
(Luke 12:7)

This revelation has captured my imagination as I've learned more of God's big plan. Just think...Jesus Christ has fulfilled over 300 prophecies through His birth, life and resurrection.

What confidence we have in every word yet to be fulfilled.

Lord, you are my God;
I will exalt you and praise your name,
for in perfect faithfulness
you have done wonderful things,
things planned long ago.
(Isaiah 25:1)

This truth became so real on my mission trip to the Ukraine. My dear friend, Nela, invited me to teach Bible Storying to pastors and women ministering to families through Mission to Ukraine. I was touched by the dedication and love shown to many precious hurting and needy men, women and children.

Jesus reached out through the loving efforts of each servant of God I met. His stories were healing to many hearts as they learned to tell them. One day we had the privilege to join a Messianic Jewish Pastor who ministered to Holocaust Survivors, who were very poor and destitute. Through food, distributing supplies and personal visits to their homes, we experienced such blessing.

These precious Jewish survivors had been through so much suffering and loss. We prayed earnestly that we could bring hope and healing to their hearts and lives. After ministering to them for three years, the Jewish believing pastor was discouraged. He grieved their loss of even believing in God and their hopelessness but kept on praying and serving them.

183

God spoke to us through His Holy Word, as we prayed He led us to the Book of Ezekiel where the prophet asks,

> *"Son of man, can these bones live?"*
> *I said, "Sovereign Lord, you alone know."*
> (Ezekiel 37:3)

It was as if the Lord was telling us, Yes they can come to life, even though their hopes and dreams have died. Pastor Arkady invited them to a special lunch where he first shared the Word of God with them.

As Nela and I sat there praying, I looked into their hopeless faces and an overwhelming compassion and sorrow came over me for what they had been through. Tears streamed down my cheeks.

Unexpectedly, the pastor invited me to come to share with these dear people. All I could do was fall to my knees before them as the Holy Spirit came upon me. I humbled myself before them and asked for their forgiveness for what was done to them in the name of Christianity." I shared how much God loved them and longed for them to know Him. Through Abraham, a covenant was given to them that He would bless all people. As my tears fell, I saw many of them were also crying.

Such a moving picture of the Lord's great compassion to reveal His love to them! I reminded them of the unconditional promise of God in Zechariah 8 yet to be fulfilled. God had not forgotten them, but the best was yet to come.

> *This is what the Lord Almighty says: "I will save*
> *my people from the countries of the east and the west.*
> *I will bring them back to live in Jerusalem;*
> *they will be my people, and I will*
> *be faithful and righteous to them as their God."*
> (Zechariah 8:7-8)

I then told them that Jesus (Yeshua) was a Jew who came for them and I am forever grateful to the Jewish people for receiving God's plan and being a part of His covenant.

I then felt led to invite the Jewish pastor to come and lead them in prayer. It was truly a divine moment when their eyes and hearts were open to see who Jesus (Yeshua) was and is for them... their Messiah and Savior. Every one of them came forward to receive Him as their own Messiah. My heart was in awe of God's miracle of salvation as He opened their blind eyes to clearly see Him for who He really is!

That day the window of my soul was opened to see the heart of God for His chosen people who have suffered so much. They are the people God chose to bring forth His Promised Savior and Messiah who came for all people, whether Jew or Gentile from every nation and ethnicity. He loves people of all faith backgrounds and longs to reveal the Glory of His Story to each one. One day soon He will return to earth to reclaim His Kingdom.

On that day living water will flow out from Jerusalem,
half of it east to the Dead Sea and half of it west to the
Mediterranean Sea, in summer and in winter.
The Lord will be king over the whole earth. On that day
there will be one Lord, and his name the only name.
(Zechariah 14:8-9)

Our story can be a part of completing His love story as we embrace Him as our Savior and King. For together, all believers in Yeshua (Jesus) make up the Bride of Messiah. We are then entrusted with a holy commission.

The Spirit and the bride say, "Come!" And let the one who
hears say, "Come!" Let the one who is thirsty come; and
let the one who wishes take the free gift of the water of life.
(Revelation 22:17)

Personal Reflection

Read the story of the beggar and the rich man in Luke 16:19-31.

Reflect on considering both of these men. They each have a story of their life on earth and eternal life. Do you know for certain You will spend eternity in the presence of God? Consider these promises in the Word of God:

You make known to me the path of life; you will fill me with joy in your presence, with eternal pleasures at your right hand. (Psalm 16:11)

For God so loved the world that he gave his one and only Son, that whoever believes in him shall not perish but have eternal life. (John 3:16)

And this is the testimony: God has given us eternal life, and this life is in His Son. (1 John 5:11)

Respond by knowing the gift of eternal life is a costly. Jesus purchased for each of us on the cross by dying in our place. If you have never opened your heart to receive this precious gift, you can today. Whatever your background, God love you and offers you eternal life.

Pray "Jesus, I need You! Please forgive me for running my own life. I want to repent of my sins and turn to You. Please come into my life as You promised and make me Your child now and forever." (2 Corinthians 9:15).

Praise Jesus for His gift to You! Your eternal story begins when you become a child of God. He is the author of your story which is being written "for His glory". Share it with others who still need to know His awesome and eternal gift. Remember to pray for the precious Jewish people who still need to discover Yeshua (Jesus) as their Messiah.

My Wall of Fire

Blazing love pierces my heart,
Beckoning me to a new start;

I cannot contain the fire within,
Surrendering any stain of sin;

Mercy shown on the cross,
Overshadows any loss;

Mighty God, Protector and King,
All praise and honor I bring;

Jealous love, blazing fire,
You are my sole desire;

Surrounded by Your fire wall,
I hear Your passionate call;

You alone are my glory,
The author of our love story!

Your Beloved Bride,
Sweet Jerusalem, the Apple of Your Eye

"And I myself will be a wall of fire around it, declares the
Lord, and I will be its glory within."
(Zechariah 2:5)

Name Above All Names

God invites you into His eternal love story!

ℳame ℳbove ℳll ℳames

Writing this book and recording His divine encounters has resulted in only a small picture of the King of All.

I am captivated by our Awesome and Extravagant God who left His throne of Glory to pursue each of us.

His miraculous humble birth and life shows the depth of His love and His desire for every precious person to know Him.

Therefore God exalted him to the highest place and gave him the name that is above every name, that at the name of Jesus every knee should bow, in heaven and on earth and under the earth, and every tongue acknowledge that Jesus Christ is Lord, to the glory of God the Father.
(Philippians 2:9-11)

Jesus' heart is one of love and compassion shown through His death on the cross, to pay the debt of ours sins. He shed His blood on the cross for our sinful hearts. When the soldiers put spikes into His hands and feet and they pierced His side with a spear, His heart also bled for us. God says,

Without the shedding of blood there is no remission of sin.
(Hebrews 9:22)

And now God says, "I commend My love toward you, that while you were sinners, Christ died for you."
(based on Romans 5:8)

God made him who had no sin to be sin for us, so that in him we might become the righteousness of God.
(2 Corinthians 5:21)

This demonstration of His love is such an amazing gift that none of us can fully grasp.

Because of His resurrection, we have the assurance of our salvation. Yet, so many do not know of this radical Love of God.

*To Him who loves us and has freed us from our sins by His
blood, and has made us to be a kingdom and priests to serve His
God and Father—to Him be glory and power for ever and ever!
"Look, he is coming with the clouds," and "every eye will see
Him, even those who pierced him"; and all peoples on earth
"will mourn because of him." So shall it be! Amen.*
(Revelation 1:6-7)

There is an urgency in my spirit to declare His glory, as He prepares to come again to this earth to establish His Kingdom.

*For the earth will be filled with the knowledge of the
glory of the Lord as the waters cover the sea.*
(Habakkuk 2:14)

Walking and praying on the beach one day, my mind was stretched to think about this promise. Every promise of God will be fulfilled as already over 300 prophecies of Jesus have been fulfilled exactly as foretold. We could be the final generation that sees this promise and others fulfilled completely.

*"And this gospel of the kingdom will be preached in the whole
world as a testimony to all nations,
and then the end will come."*
(Matthew 24:14)

Until then, we have the greatest joy and privilege to complete Jesus rescue Mission of mankind! Just as the first disciples received the gift of the Holy Spirit, we too are commanded to "be filled with the Holy Spirit," the Father's gift to us. After Jesus rose from the dead before He ascended into heaven He told His disciples...

*"Do not leave Jerusalem, but wait for the gift my Father
promised, which you have heard me speak about.
For John baptized with water, but in a few days you will be
baptized with the Holy Spirit. But you will receive power when
the Holy Spirit comes on you; and you will be my witnesses in
Jerusalem, and in all Judea and Samaria,
and to the ends of the earth."*
(Acts 1:4-5;8)

As you read the account in Acts 2, you see the fulfillment of Jesus' promise. In one moment these once fearful disciples were empowered with boldness to speak forth the Word of God in other tongues. On that day, 3,000 new believers received the message of salvation through Jesus and were baptized.

We can never accomplish this on our own. Jesus did not leave us on our own but gave us the gift of His Holy Spirit to live in and through us. You can be filled with the Holy Spirit by faith and experience God's supernatural guidance and power every moment.

One day soon, He will create a new earth where He will reign forever and ever with those who receive His invitation!

> *He will wipe every tear from their eyes.*
> *There will be no more death or mourning*
> *or crying or pain, for the old order*
> *of things has passed away.*
> *He who was seated on the throne said,*
> *"I am making everything new!"*
> (Revelation 21:4-5a)

I'm waiting on tip toes for this day. How about you, my friend? Why not seal your place with Him right now?

The Holy Spirit is our power source to fulfill Jesus' Mission! Pray with me...

Dear Father God, I need You. I acknowledge that I have sinned against You by directing my own life. I thank You that You have forgiven my sins through Christ's death on the cross for me. I now invite Christ to again take His place on the throne of my life. Fill me with the Holy Spirit as You commanded me to be filled, and as You promised in Your Word that You would do if I asked in faith. I pray this in the name of Jesus. I now thank You for filling me with the Holy Spirit and directing my life.

His Names

If I begin to name the names of my God, it will be established that there is none like Him. What name shall we call Him, the one who has revealed Himself in so many ways? For He is the Creator, He is Jehovah, He is the Father, He is the Son, He is the Holy Spirit. His names reveal His power, His wisdom, His holiness, His justice, His truth, His loving-kindness, His ineffable, measureless wonder. His name is Wonderful, Counselor, the Mighty God, the Everlasting Father, the Prince of Peace. He is the Rose of Sharon, the Lily of the Valley, the Bright and Morning Star. He is the fairest of ten thousand, the Alpha and the Omega; the Beginning and the End, the First and the Last. He is the Most High God, possessor of Heaven and earth. He is the eternal God, He is Almighty God, He is Redeemer, and Lord. He is the shadow of a rock in a weary land. He is our light and salvation; our fortress and our high tower.

Oh, let me boast in my God, for there is none like unto Him. He is the Ancient of Days, seated upon the throne of Heaven. He is the Man of Sorrow walking upon the earth, He is Elohim, the Father of Eternity and He is the babe of Bethlehem. He is the Way, the Truth and the Life, He is the Light of the World; the Bread of Life; the Good Shepherd that giveth His life for the sheep. O let me boast in my God. There is none like unto Him. He is the water of life, the living vine, the living bread from Heaven. He is the door by which we enter Heaven and He is the resurrection that shall take us out of our earth and into life eternal. O let me boast in my God for there is none like Him.

He is divine providence, the author and finisher of our faith. He is the provider for all our needs. He is our shield and our exceeding great reward. He is the Lord God of Hosts, the God of Abraham, the God of Isaac and the God of Jacob. He is not ashamed to be called their God and mine. O let me boast in the Lord, my God. for there is none like Him. He is the God of Heaven and the man of Galilee. He is the God of gods and the Lord of lords, the King of kings." (Compiled from the Bible by Donald Grey)

Let us all boast in the Lord our God, for truly there is NONE like unto Him.

Your Name

You came down in a cloud,
Moses, covered in a shroud;
Passing in front, calling out,
With a holy shout!
"Yahweh! The Lord!
The God of compassion and mercy.
"I am slow to anger and filled with unfailing love
and faithfulness." (Exodus 34:6 NLT)
Moses worshipped You.
O Lord, if it is true,
That favor I have found.
Please let Your presence abound;
Forgive our iniquity and sin,
And all our evil within;
Claim us as Your own,
May Your Glory be shown.
The Lord replied,
as Moses sighed.
"I am making a covenant with you,
in the presence of all your people too."
Miracles will be displayed,
As you have prayed.
Awesome power for all to see,
This will be from ME!
Listen carefully and obey,
Follow only My way.
My name is Jealous,
for you I am zealous.
For you and your people are Mine,
Chosen and set apart to shine.
Later God sent His own Son,
Declaring all the work is done.
His precious blood was shed,
For His Bride to wed...
Her Savior, Prince and King.

Flourishing Like a Palm Tree

P alm trees are stately strong and stunning. They survive storms and drought, for their roots go down deep. Living in Florida, I love to see their beauty and the needed shade they provide.

How profound it is, that the Psalms describe lovers of God as ones who flourish like palm trees.

Over the years, my greatest heroes are those whom I see "thriving" as they grow in "victory" and "stand with strength."

Corrie Ten Boom is a heroine to me, as she survived a German concentration camp for hiding Jews during the Holocaust. One day before she would have been executed, she was miraculously released, after losing her entire family in the death camps. She became a "Tramp for the Lord," as she describes in her book. Her influence impacted nations, as she spoke on forgiveness and hope in the midst of such evil.

"No pit is so deep, that the love of God is not deeper still," she proclaimed everywhere she went. Corrie shared her story, along with the glorious Gospel of Jesus Christ until she went home to be with Him at age 91.

So many heroes to me are seasoned saints, who overflowed with the Lord's presence and anointing.

George Joslin, who in his 90s was still preaching the Gospel in prison crusades. He didn't miss one opportunity to share Jesus love and truth with everyone he met.

Dr. Bill Bright, who declared, "I don't believe in retirement; but instead to be 'Refired' for His Kingdom!" First love for Jesus "compelled him to share God's Love Story with everyone He met."

Precious Pearl who traveled the world reaching children with Jesus love. She became an inspiration, example and faithful prayer partner, until she went to heaven at 100 years of age. So many more, who inspired and impacted me greatly.

But one special man, was my very own dad. Dad was a hard worker, determined and competent man in business and sports.

He succeeded in football and baseball, playing in the minor leagues for the St. Louis Browns, before they became the Cardinals. Wow!

I always looked up to him. His love, was shown through his actions and faithfulness to his children and to mom, who had ten years of Alzheimer's. He lovingly cared for her and honored his love and marriage covenant.

When I shared with dad that I met Jesus personally, after having a wonderful Christian upbringing, he didn't understand at first. But, I'm forever grateful that he gave me his blessing, and over time was proud of his crazy, Jesus loving, missionary daughter, even though he didn't fully get it. I prayed earnestly and believed for dad to understand and receive Jesus as His personal Savior.

My greatest of all memories of Dad came at age 85, when he was dying from kidney failure. I had asked Jesus for a Christmas present; to know beyond a shadow of doubt that Dad would be in heaven.

So one night, before Christmas I asked him, "Dad, if I come back to see you tomorrow and you are not here, are you going to be in heaven?"

"I hope so." He said. "That's not good enough, Dad," I urgently replied, "The Lord Jesus wants you to know for sure. He promises *"Whoever has God's Son has life; whoever does not have His Son, does not have life.' I have written this to you who believe in the Son of God so that you may know you have eternal life. "* (John 5:12-13)

"Don't you think it is time to put a stake in the ground and make this decision?" I asked. Immediately he agreed. And like a child, he humbled himself to admit his sin and receive Jesus as His Savior and Lord through a simple prayer.

I'm forever grateful that now I'll spend all eternity in the glorious Kingdom of Heaven with my precious Dad and my entire family who have received Jesus as their Savior!

How about you? Are you sure of your salvation? Or is it time to settle your eternal destiny? To lead your family or someone you love to Him. Now is the time!

For he says, "In the time of my favor I heard you, and in the day of salvation I helped you." I tell you, now is the time of God's favor, now is the day of salvation.
(2 Corinthians 6:2)

Poured Out Love

My Beloved, so pure and holy
Made Himself weak and lowly;

Surrendered His glory,
To begin our love story!

All creation under a curse.
He alone could reverse;

Purchase price so high,
Lamb of God had to die;

Cup of sufferings real,
Bread broken as a seal,

Father turned away,
On that fateful day;

Jesus carried the weight of sin,
All our selfish pride within;

Every heartache, pain and loss,
He carried on that cross;

Covenant love in His blood,
Poured out as a flood,

Washing away the wall,
Every knee will one day fall;

King Jesus conquered and arose!
Everyone on earth knows,

Love so amazing, so divine.
Jesus, Savior, King is mine!

Priceless Pearl

After I personally met Jesus, my life began to take on a new purpose. It was clear He was calling me to invest my life in sharing His love and truth with teenagers and everyone else. Dad was not prepared for this, neither was Mom. Lots of conversations followed and with God's gracious love, they gave me their blessing, without fully understanding.

So Dad being the provider he always was, decided he should cash in my life insurance to give me the money. Wow!

"Why don't you take the money and buy a ring?" he suggested.

"Dad, that is so kind of you. Yes!" I exclaimed. What a treat, since I was just graduating from college.

Praying to find just the right ring as I went to the store, I headed to the jewelry department. There it was! Immediately the beautiful single pearl, surrounded with gold leaves captured my imagination.

"This is the ring," I announced excitedly to the sweet young sales girl.

"Do you know about the Pearl?" I added. "The pearl of great price."

She looked confused, "I don't think so. Tell me."

What joy it was to tell Jessica the precious parable Jesus told about the Kingdom of God:

"The kingdom of heaven is like treasure hidden in a field.
When a man found it, he hid it again, and then in his joy went
and sold all he had and bought that field.
Again, the kingdom of heaven is like a merchant
looking for fine pearls. When he found one of great value,
he went away and sold everything he had and bought it."
(Matthew 13:44-46)

"You see, Jessica, I found the pearl of great price; and His name is Jesus. Do you know Him?" I eagerly asked.

"I don't think I know Him like you do" she responded."

With joy I shared how she, too, could receive the priceless gift of Jesus. He gave His life on the cross to purchase us with His blood. Clearly, she was touched by the Holy Spirit, as she prayed with me to receive His gift of forgiveness of sins and eternal life.

My friend, I invite you today to open your heart and soul to Jesus, today, and begin Your eternal life now, if you have never before done so.

Simply pray with me . . .

Lord Jesus, I need You. Thank You for dying on the cross in my place for my sins. I believe in You and I open the door of my life and receive You as my Savior and Lord. Thank You for forgiving me of my sins and giving me eternal life. Take control of the throne of my life and make me the kind of person You want me to be.

If you prayed this prayer, He has heard your heartfelt prayer and come into your life. You are His new creation.

Therefore, if anyone is in Christ, the new creation has come:
The old has gone, the new is here!
*(*2 Corinthians 5:17)

I invite you to share the priceless Pearl Jesus with everyone you know and even with those you do not know. He can use you to tell them. He knows each one by name, just as He knows and loves you. You are embarking on an eternal adventure as you embrace your role in His eternal love story!

It has only just begun...

Eternal Love Story

I looked for a Prince and
Found the King.

A love story that
Makes my heart sing.

He chose me before the world began,
And through His love prepared a plan;

That I would finally know,
And be one to show;

His majesty and glory,
The wonder of His story.

Intimacy beyond compare,
A heavenly love affair;

Meant for me to share,
Love, truth and care;

For a world in desperation,
Longing for hope and salvation;

Yeshua is His Name,
No one the same.

Salvation is why He came,
Not for glory or fame.

The Father gave His mission,
He chose full submission;

He sacrificed and died,
Satan's power was defied;

When He burst forth alive,
The Messiah did arrive.

Hallelujah to our King.
Salvation, He did bring.

Awaiting our wedding day,
His Beloved Bride.

He Invites You by Name

W hat a privilege, my friend, to have you take this journey with me. It has been my prayer that you will be captivated by the lover of your soul! He who created you desires to spend eternity with you!

Just as a wedding invitation must be accepted with a reservation, so you must respond to God's invitation! As I faced my Stage 4 Ovarian Cancer diagnosis, suddenly the reality of death and eternity was clear. What a joy and hope, to know that whatever happened, my eternal destiny was secure. My life belongs to my "Everlasting Father".

For to us a child is born, to us a son is given,
and the government will be on his shoulders.
And he will be called Wonderful Counselor, Mighty God,
Everlasting Father, Prince of Peace.
(Isaiah 9:6)

Studying the Word of God, I see that many prophecies have been fulfilled, just as were told! Over 300 prophecies about Jesus have been fulfilled exactly, and some of the most exciting are still to come in His perfect time. Jesus Himself comforted His disciples on the eve of His death, with these words:

"And if I go and prepare a place for you, I will come back and take you to be with me that you also may be where I am."
(John 14:3)

He promised he would come again to bring them to their future home being prepared by himself. After his death and resurrection they were with him, after He had appeared to over 500 eyewitnesses. Giving them instructions to be His witnesses and wait for the power of the Holy Spirit, they then watched as he ascended into heaven.

They were looking intently up into the sky as he was going, when suddenly two men dressed in white stood beside them. "Men of Galilee," they said, "why do you stand here looking into the sky? This same Jesus, who has been taken from you into heaven, will

come back in the same way you have seen him go into heaven."
(Acts 1:10-11)

Don't you want to know more of what that means? Read the final chapters in the book of Revelation, and you will discover his plans that are unfolding in our generation. His words give us an expectancy and urgency to be in step with His purpose and plan.

"Look, I am coming soon! My reward is with me,
and I will give to each person according to what they have done.
I am the Alpha and the Omega, the First and the Last,
the Beginning and the End."
(Revelation 22:12-13)

God Himself invites you into His eternal love story! He has an honored and unique role for each of us who receive His invitation...We are called "His Bride"! As His "Beloved Bride" we share his heart, his passion and purposes forever! Could anything be more awesome than this?

The Spirit and the bride say, "Come!" And let the
one who hears say, "Come!" Let the one who is thirsty come;
and let the one who wishes take the free gift of the water of life.

He who testifies to these things says, "Yes, I am coming soon."
(Revelation 22;17, 20)

As the days grow darker, I am on "TIP TOES" waiting for His trumpet call, signaling His coming for His "Beloved Bride!"

For the Lord himself will come down from heaven,
with a loud command, with the voice of the archangel
and with the trumpet call of God, and the
dead in Christ will rise first. After that, we who are
still alive and are left will be caught up together with t
hem in the clouds to meet the Lord in the air.
And so we will be with the Lord forever.
Therefore encourage one another with these words.
(1 Thessalonians 4:16-18)

Praying I will spend eternity with you, my dear friend.
Love in Jesus,

Nancy

Resources by Nancy Wilson

Chosen With A Mission: Are You Ready for the Adventure?

Delightfully entertaining, practical and inspirational. *Chosen With A Mission* sizzles with Nancy's real-life adventures while presenting a solid blueprint and a study guide for understanding and fulfilling the unique mission God has for each of us. You will discover possibilities of the Christian life from God's Word and His work in Nancy's life.

The King and I

The King and I captures the passion of an intimate relationship with Jesus Christ in a unique and moving fashion. Have you wondered what it actually means to be the Bride of Christ? Nancy leads you into His presence as you embrace a fresh love relationship with King Jesus, the lover of your soul.

In Pursuit of the Ideal

In Pursuit of the Ideal is a timely book written to a generation that needs, above everything, to know the identity and worth with which each one in that generation it has been created. What would you like to be prettier, thinner, smarter? That is what the world presses you to be. But what is the true ideal and how can you ever achieve it? Nancy explores these questions and helps you find the answers you have been searching for. The answers may surprise you!

For information on ordering these books or finding out more about Nancy's ministry go to www.nancywilson.org.

SPEAKING MINISTRY:

Nancy dynamically communicates the truth of Jesus Christ to the heart issues of this generation with conviction and compassion. She has a zeal for evangelism and spiritual awakening. Her desire is to ignite fresh love and passion for Jesus (through outreach events, training, conferences and retreats). Her speaking topics appeal to various ages and cultures through motivating them to be a part of fulfilling God's mission.

Go to www.nancywilson.org to see more themes and topics.

EVANGELISM TRAINING:

The Glory of God's Story

Israel...the place where God's eternal love story comes alive! Have you been there or dreamed of going? Nancy invites you to experience *His Story* as it unfolds in Israel. Travel withher as she tells God's story and engages people with *His Story.* go to www.nancywilson.org to learnmore.

• **StoryWave** Evangelism training (see the next few pages)

CHOSEN WITH A MISSION MINISTRY:

Nancy has a passion to raise up young world changers, and has many spiritual children around the world! She is the Patron Mother for: Chosen Junior School for orphans, the poor and needy in Matugga, Uganda. James Kintu, her beloved spiritual son, is the Director, and Pastor of Grace and Glory Chapel.

Go to www.chosenwithamission.org to learn more.

TUMAINI JEWELS INTITIATIVE:

This mission of hope has been launched in Mombasa, Kenya by Nancy and her spiritual daughter, Maureen. Once an orphan, she is now a godly young woman who has a heart for precious young girls who have been orphaned or abused. Our vision is to rescue, redeem and restore these jewels for His glory!

StoryWave Training

For the earth will be filled with the knowledge of the glory of the Lord as the waters cover the sea. (Habakkuk 2:14)

Catching the wave of God's Spirit by unleashing the power of telling God's story and creatively connecting to the heart of this generation as we capture the momentum of God's mission and movement.

Every culture and generation must search for the must effective way to connect people's hearts to God's heart. Just as Jesus knew His audience and taught in ways that they could relate to, we will explore various oral means of communication in relating the never changing eternal love story of the Gospel.

Two-thirds of the world's population are oral learners who simply prefer to learn and process life in a narrative experiential way. StoryWave training offers an innovative storying approach that employs people's heart language and learning style. This training integrates storying into evangelism, discipleship and missions strategy.

Training Content

- story telling basics
- StoryWave evangelism connecting through story, addressing felt need issues through story and learning to tell your story with God's story
- learning creative ways to tell God's story (drama, media song/dance, arts)
- crafting stories for your specific audience
- learning how to begin a story group
- exploring strategy in mission

Come and Learn

- How to tell Bible stories. Evangelize, disciple and reach-out in short term missions.
- Be equipped to connect with the heart of this generation. Connect your story with God's story.
- Experience the joy and power of Bible Storying in a small group.
- Explore creative ways to disciple and share Jesus with others more effectively.

I praise God for the opportunity He gave us to connect with Nancy and the special ministry of StoryWave training. This ministry teaches us how to present Jesus' story's and bring them alive in people's lives! It has been the most successful activity in our 18 years of ministry in Colombia, S.A. We serve the Lord with Open Arms Church and Boys Recovery House.

At the boy's recovery house, it was a problem finding a way to present God's love to these kids who have been abused, neglected by the society, family and peers, but with the StoryWave methodology they just love it! For the first time in many years we believe they are understanding the Gospel and the love of God!

At the church we are using it in many ways... at the Sunday School for children and adolescents, they are motivated to be part of stories, at home Bible studies, family meetings, and in their workplaces, they learn the story and then shared it with others.

I praise God and thank the StoryWave ministry, under Nancy Wilson that had bought this new methodology to present the Gospel! May many more people learn about it!

—Enoc and Christian Hernandez, Open Arms Ministry
Colombia, South America

Nancy Wilson is a dynamic speaker and author who combines a zest for life and people. She has over 40 years of ministry experience. After serving for 25 years, as Associate National Director of Cru High School ministry and International Director for 10 years, she now serves as Global Ambassador for Cru and leads StoryWave Evangelism Training.
Nancy travels extensively and is a frequent speaker to audiences of all ages in the U.S. and Internationally. As Global Ambassador for Cru she has ministered in 77 countries. Her passion is to "lift up Jesus" as she leads retreats, conferences and training for diverse audiences i.e. men and women, churches and youth.

When not traveling, Nancy resides in Florida and her extended family lives in St. Louis, Missouri. She has four brothers and one sister and is a proud aunt of nineteen precious nieces and nephews. Also, a blessed spiritual mother to many around the world including Chosen with a Mission School for orphans and needy founded by her beloved spiritual son, James Kintu.

Fun Trivia: As a former dolphin trainer, Nancy loves to visit nearby beaches and swim in the ocean with dolphins!
Nancy hosts a radio show, StoryWave...Ripples of Radical Love to Rock your World. You can listen to programs on ***www.artistfirst.com/nancywilson.htm***

To arrange for Nancy Wilson to speak at your event. host a training or for further information contact her at:

100 Lake Hart Drive, Dept. 1100 • Orlando, FL 32832
(407) 443-7720
Email: *nancy.wilson@cru.org*
You can learn more on her website: *www.nancywilson.org*